Praise for
Why God Won't Go Away

"Above the clamor of today's competing ideologies on the supernatural comes the rigorous and robust defense of the God of the Bible by Dr. McGrath. This is a book for serious thinkers who wish to make God real in a world that has forgotten its Creator and Maker. Absorb its insights, then pass it on to those who are hungry for more than this world can give!"

—Joni Eareckson Tada,
Author, *A Place of Healing*
Joni and Friends International Disability Center

"In this accessible, easy-to-read and easy-to-follow book, McGrath makes a persuasive case for the demise within recent time of the New Atheism. A natural extension of his public debates with the likes of Richard Dawkins and Christopher Hitchens, McGrath brings to this volume not only his usual academic clarity but also a charming, almost courtly manner that does honor to him, his argument, and us as his readers."

—Phyllis Tickle
Author, *The Great Emergence*

"In this compellingly readable expose of the movement, Alister McGrath introduces its main proponents, dissects its claims, and assesses its prognosis. It is beautifully and clearly written. But although he is entertaining, McGrath rightly resists the temptation to be *merely* entertaining. The temptation must have been great. But it would have been at the expense of the book's primary trait—its passionate and infectious humility. McGrath sees, as few Christian apologists do, that the New Atheists' main mistake is their fundamentalism, and their consequent blindness to the possibility of looking at this extraordinary Universe in ways other than their own.

"The New Atheism may well be an ephemeral movement, but this should not be an ephemeral book. Its lasting value is not that it is a splendid anatomy of the New Atheism (although it is), but that it holds up to Christians an often discomforting mirror; that it forces us to distinguish between proselytism and respectful, truly mutual conversation; and that it might persuade Christians to look for the truth, wherever it may lie."

—Charles Foster
Fellow of Green Templeton College, University of Oxford
Author, *The Selfless Gene, The Sacred Journey,* and *The Jesus Inquest*

WHY GOD WON'T GO AWAY

IS THE NEW ATHEISM RUNNING ON EMPTY?

WHY GOD WON'T GO AWAY

ALISTER MCGRATH

THOMAS NELSON
Since 1798

NASHVILLE   DALLAS   MEXICO CITY   RIO DE JANEIRO

Published in Nashville, Tennessee, by Thomas Nelson. Thomas Nelson is a registered trademark of Thomas Nelson, Inc.

Excerpts from *The God Delusion* by Richard Dawkins. Copyright © 2006 by Richard Dawkins. Reprinted by permission of Houghton Mifflin Harcourt Publishing Company. All rights reserved.

Thomas Nelson, Inc., titles may be purchased in bulk for educational, business, fund-raising, or sales promotional use. For information, please e-mail SpecialMarkets@ThomasNelson.com.

All Scripture quotations are taken from HOLY BIBLE: NEW INTERNATIONAL VERSION®. © 1973, 1978, 1984 by International Bible Society. Used by permission of Zondervan Publishing House. All rights reserved.

Page design by Mark L. Mabry

Library of Congress Cataloging-in-Publication Data

McGrath, Alister E., 1953-
  Why god won't go away : is the new atheism running on empty? / Alister McGrath.
    p. cm.
  Includes bibliographical references (pp. 153–56).
  ISBN 978-0-8499-4645-5 (pbk.)
  1. Apologetics. 2. Christianity and atheism. I. Title.
  BT1212.M34 2011
  239'.7--dc22
  2010052474

Printed in the United States of America

11 12 13 14 15 RRD 9 8 7 6 5 4 3 2 1

For Bruce and Phyllis Beard

Contents

INTRODUCTION

In September 2001, a series of coordinated suicide attacks was launched against targets in the United States—events now referred to simply as 9/11. Of the four planes hijacked by Islamic terrorists, three were flown into major landmark buildings in New York and Washington, D.C., causing considerable loss of life. The impact of these attacks was massive, reflecting a widespread perception that the world had just changed irreversibly. The "war against terror" became a dominant theme of the presidency of George W. Bush, and the United States and its allies became enmeshed in conflicts in Iraq and Afghanistan. Public anxiety about the deadly consequences of religious fanaticism reached new levels.

In the view of many, this last point is of critical importance for understanding the sudden emergence in the first decade of the twenty-first century of the movement now known as the New Atheism.[1] Some atheist writers, such as Richard Dawkins, had been arguing for years that religion was irrational and dangerous, without making much headway. Suddenly these atheist arguments seemed both attractive and culturally plausible. Someone or something had to be blamed for 9/11, and Islamic religious fanaticism was an obvious possibility. In the white heat of anger against this outrage, *Islamic religious fanaticism* became simplified—first to *religious fanaticism* and then simply to *religion*.

Dawkins would play a central role in this change in cultural mood in Western liberal circles, for 9/11 confirmed everything he'd always believed: religion was dangerous precisely because it was irrational, and when it failed to win arguments, it resorted to terror instead. Four days after the attack, Dawkins wrote, "to fill a world with religion, or religions of the Abrahamic kind, is like littering the streets with loaded guns. Do not be surprised if they are used."[2]

Many regarded these comments as ridiculously simplistic. Others, however, saw Dawkins as a bold thinker willing to tell the truth. Religion is dangerous. It's not to be respected but to be feared—and wherever possible, neutralized. It's a time bomb waiting to explode, a loaded gun waiting to kill people. As Christopher Hitchens put the point a few years later, with a verbal economy matched only by its emotional intensity, "Religion kills." The 9/11 attack turned out to be the intellectual and moral launchpad for the New Atheism.

If the New Atheism wanted to get a debate about religion

under way, it certainly succeeded. Suddenly everyone wanted to talk about God. I and many others have welcomed this debate. The New Atheism has raised questions of fundamental importance, such as the rationality of faith, the relation of religion and science, the possible links between faith and violence, and the place of religion in Western society. For many years, these matters were seen as uninteresting and irrelevant. But not now. A most interesting conversation has begun, and I'm sure the New Atheism will not mind others joining in and taking the discussion further. There's a lot more that needs to be said.

Why? Because God just won't go away. In the UK, the influential magazine the *Economist*, which had been "so confident of the Almighty's demise that we published His obituary in our millennium issue," rather inconveniently found itself obliged to issue a correction in 2007. Religion is back in public life and public debate.[3] Many are now wondering whether the New Atheism itself is beginning to look and sound a little stale and weary, repeating old arguments dressed up as if they were new and radical.

This book engages the ideas of the New Atheism, primarily as we find it stated in the works of its four leading representatives: Richard Dawkins, Daniel Dennett, Sam Harris, and Christopher Hitchens. But it's important not to limit our discussion to these four thinkers. One of the most distinctive features of the New Atheism is the virtual community it has generated. How are its ideas defended and propagated through Web sites and blogs? How do these help us understand the agendas and anxieties of the movement and its appeal to society as a whole?

We'll return to these questions in due course. First, let us chart the rise to prominence of the New Atheism and try to identify its distinctive features.

PART ONE

WHAT IS THE
NEW ATHEISM?

1

THE NEW ATHEISM: HOW IT ALL STARTED

The term *New Atheism* was invented in 2006. Gary Wolf was writing an article for *Wired*, a British magazine aimed at "smart, intellectually curious people who need, and want, to know what's next." Wolf was looking around for a snappy slogan to refer to a group of three men who'd attracted media attention through best-selling popular books advocating atheism: Sam Harris with *The End of Faith* (2004),[1] Richard Dawkins with *The God Delusion* (2006),[2] and Daniel Dennett with *Breaking the Spell* (2006).[3] The authors were already linked through a number of groups, most notably John Brockman's Edge network, which describes its purpose as "to arrive at the edge of the world's knowledge, seek out the most complex and sophisticated minds, put them in a room together, and have them ask each other the questions they are asking themselves."[4] Wolf hit on the phrase *New Atheism* to designate the approach of Dawkins, Harris, and Dennett—an enthusiastic advocation of atheism and a scathing criticism of both religious belief and cultural respect for religion.[5]

In 2007, the New Atheism movement gained a new hero when Christopher Hitchens's *God Is Not Great* became the latest atheist best seller.[6] The phrase *the Four Horsemen* began to be used to refer to these writers, who rapidly assumed celebrity status and are now collectively identified as the intellectual and cultural spearhead of the New Atheism.[7]

But who are they? Where are they coming from? What are their agendas? Before engaging with the core ideas of the New Atheism in detail, it makes sense to find out more about its four main protagonists and the approaches they develop in their books. We'll begin by considering Sam Harris (born 1967), whose *The End of Faith* is widely regarded as laying the groundwork for the rather more significant later volumes by Dawkins and Hitchens.

SAM HARRIS

In *The End of Faith* (2004), the hitherto unknown American author Sam Harris mounted a powerful rhetorical attack on religion, seeing it as the primary cause of the catastrophe of

9/11. The book bristles with anger. How could such an outrage take place in a rational nation like the United States? What does the persistence of religion tell us about the state of the human mind? What can be done to purge the nation of the dangerous delusion that there is a God?

While conceding that militant Islam must be acknowledged as the immediate cause of 9/11, Harris is nonetheless scathing of Islam as a whole: "It is not merely that we are at war with an otherwise peaceful religion that has been 'hijacked' by extremists. We are at war with precisely the vision of life that is prescribed to all Muslims."[8] But Christianity and Judaism, he believes, also deserve blame for this disaster because the problem lies with religion as such, rather than any specific form of religion. Fanatical Islam is simply a particularly extreme example of the irrationality and dysfunctionality of religious faith. The world would be a better place if no one believed in God at all.

Note that Harris's primary concern in *The End of Faith* is not to defend atheism but rather to portray religion as dangerous and deluded. Ideas that should be regarded as symptoms of mental illness—such as praying—are tolerated in Western culture simply because we've gotten used to them. Religious moderates blind society to the danger of religious extremists. The problem is not extremism or fanaticism as such but religion, which engenders such attitudes in the first place.

I read *The End of Faith* with mixed feelings back in 2005. I completely agree with Harris when he declares that religion can be a problem. It's one of the reasons I myself was an atheist when I was younger. Growing up in Northern Ireland during the 1960s, I was painfully aware of the tensions between Protestants and Catholics, and it seemed obvious that if there were no religion, there would be no religious violence. Getting rid of religion would be the key to human progress and social cohesion. In fact, as I read Harris, I felt rather nostalgic for the certainties of my youth: religion was for losers, idiots, and terrorists. Of course this is a hopelessly simplistic view that cannot be sustained in the light of subsequent scholarly research. But it was how I perceived things then.

The End of Faith has won plaudits from enthusiastic atheists, who often express delight that Harris has broken one of the fundamental taboos of American culture: the need to be respectful about religion. It needed to be ridiculed, and Harris slammed it. Yet even a casual reading of the book raises some very awkward questions. Let us look more closely, for example, at his perplexing statement that "we are at war with Islam."[9] Can this superficial critique really be sustained by the evidence? Is it not overgeneralizing to present the more fanatical elements of Islam as representative of the movement as a whole in order to justify such a war?

If the first chapter of Harris's book makes clear that he

dislikes certain forms of religion intensely, unfortunately the chapters that follow reveal that he doesn't really know very much about them. And by the end of the book, you have to wonder if the plausibility of his argument depends largely on his readers sharing his abhorrence and lack of understanding.

To his supporters, Harris is a straight talker who tells the truth. To his critics, his analysis of the question of religious violence is based on alarmist rhetoric; excessive reliance on anecdote; an appeal to popular prejudice and predisposition rather than evidence-based analysis; and above all, a failure to engage with the massive scholarly research literature on religion. He presents a highly simplistic narrative that depicts religion as the cause of the world's ills. (The weakest part of the book is a particularly unpersuasive section that invites us to believe that religion lies behind the United States' problem with drugs.) Yet his analysis is so biased and inattentive to the evidence that many are left wondering if there's a fatal disconnection here between rhetoric and reality.

Scott Atran, an anthropologist at the University of Michigan, is one mainline scholar who's worried about Harris's simplistic approach to what's clearly a complex issue. If religion causes problems, it's important to understand properly why this is so—otherwise, the solutions offered will be worthless and possibly even counterproductive. In a seminar sponsored by the Edge network, Atran launched a frontal assault on the methodology of the New Atheism. By ignoring the scholarly literature on religion, Atran declared, Harris and others were offering responses to religion that were "often scientifically baseless, psychologically uninformed, politically naive, and counterproductive."[10]

Let us agree that there are indeed some real problems about religion in the modern world and that we all need to work out what to do about them. That is why so many leading Christians talk to atheists: listening to informed criticism can help us get a sense of perspective and possibly even identify ways ahead. But I am not sure Harris really helps much here. His remedy is little more than a pastiche of prejudice and passion that aims to incite through its rhetoric as much as to persuade through its arguments. It is as if he already knows the answers and sees no point in reflecting critically on the issues. Happily for us, if inconveniently for Harris, there are more informed approaches that enable us to reflect critically yet intelligently about religion in the modern world.

A good example is Mark Juergensmeyer's important work *Terror in the Mind of God* (2000),[11] which sets out the case for believing that religion, while rarely being itself a direct cause of war and violence, can provide a potent and persuasive moral justification for violence as a form of resistance to perceived injustices and inequalities. Juergensmeyer argues that recent religious extremism reflects the failure of both secularism and modern nation states (especially the United States) to challenge and confront deprivation and injustice. It is a more complex analysis than Harris's and raises some awkward questions about the impact of US foreign policy on encouraging religious radicalization in the Islamic world. But it does seem to be based on much better evidence and to make more sense of what's happening around us.

Or again, we might consider the detailed evidence-based arguments in William Cavanaugh's recent study, *The Myth of Religious Violence* (2009).[12] Cavanaugh's book provides a sustained critique of contemporary thinkers—such as Harris—who argue that religion generates its own distinctive pathological kind of violence, which is to be distinguished from legitimate secular violence.[13] Cavanaugh argues that this is neither scholarly persuasive nor socially liberal. Harris's agenda, he concludes, is to use the false category of "religious violence" to "marginalize discourses and practices labelled 'religious.'"[14]

Harris's apparent belief that liberal society uses violence to enforce only noble values and aspirations seems more than a little naive. Many have drawn the troubling conclusion that violence does not solve anything at all, but simply creates a cycle of violence that perpetuates and amplifies the problem.

The really disturbing parts of Harris's book concern his own views, not his criticisms of religion. In one section, after rightly noting that beliefs shape behavior, he argues that "some propositions are so dangerous that it may even be ethical to kill people for believing them. This may seem an extraordinary claim, but it merely enunciates an ordinary fact about the world in which we live."[15] Killing such people, he tells us, could be regarded as an act of self-defense.

The Inquisition, the Gestapo, the Taliban, and the KGB could not have put it better.[16] To be honest, I found Harris's statement to be morally repulsive. I hope I'm right in believing that Harris does not intend his readers to draw the conclusion that if certain beliefs cause people to behave in ways society chooses to regard as dangerous, we should get rid of them—both the beliefs and the people. But his pontifications seem to open the door to those wishing to argue that since "religion generates violence and hatred" (a core New Atheist doctrine), it could be ethical to kill religious believers in order to make the world a better and safer place. I rather hope Sam Harris never becomes president of the United States! Happily, many moral atheists outside the New Atheist establishment have made clear their revulsion against Harris's dogged, even violent, intolerance of religion.[17] It's good to see that other sections of the atheist movement have a more robust moral sense than what we find in this early New Atheist manifesto.

Harris continued his criticism of religion in the briefer volume, *Letter to a Christian Nation* (2006).[18] Despite a two-hundred-thousand-dollar promotion budget, partly contributed by Harris himself,[19] this book did not have quite the impact of his original controversial best seller. More recently, in *The Moral Landscape: How Science can Determine Human Values* (2010), he argued that science is able to provide a reliable objective basis for human ethics.[20] What's been regarded as one of the most important defenses of religion—that it offers a basis for morality that's not available to reason or religion—can thus be rebutted. As we'll note later, *The Moral Landscape* turns out to be a surprisingly weak book, which defends its core thesis largely by ignoring the obvious arguments against it.

It's fair to say that Harris set the tone for the New Atheism and gave it its distinctive voice. His aggressive prose showed that there was a market for works that directly attacked religious beliefs and practices, and after *The End of Faith*, New Atheist arguments against religion generally took the form of "pseudo-refuting description" (in the words of Anthony Flew) in which a vicious account of something was assumed to be equivalent to its dismissal on rational and evidential grounds.

However, it's important not to judge the New Atheism solely by Harris's curtain-raising volume. There's much more to come.

RICHARD DAWKINS

By far the most interesting of the subsequent works advocating the New Atheism is *The God Delusion* (2006) by the British writer Richard Dawkins (born 1941). It may lack the rhetorical polish of Christopher Hitchens's later *God Is Not Great*, but it more than compensates for this by its comprehensive critique of religion and advocacy of atheism. Where Harris simply ridiculed religion, Dawkins goes much further: if there's an atheistic equivalent to C. S. Lewis's *Mere Christianity*, this is it.

From the outset, Dawkins makes it clear that he's engaged in a crusade. "If this book works as I intend," he writes, "religious readers who open it will be atheists when they put it down."[21] However, Dawkins is inclined to think that religious people are so obstinately wedded to their ridiculous beliefs that they'll hang on to them, no matter how rational the opposing case presented. In his own pithy phrase, "Dyed-in-the-wool faith-heads are immune to argument."[22] I suppose he means people like me, who used to be atheists and then decided that Christianity was really rather more interesting. And that it made a lot more sense.

So what sort of arguments does Dawkins deploy in this work? I won't be able to do justice to all his ideas here, but let us say that he sets out the main approaches that have become characteristic of the New Atheism. Unlike Harris, Dawkins does not condone the use of torture, argue that the illegal drug problem in the United States is religious in origin, or suggest that it might be moral to execute people with potentially dangerous ideas. Instead, he sets out to build a cumulative case against religion or belief in God—without making a clear or defensible distinction between them—in which a number of themes are prominent.

First, Dawkins declares that faith is fundamentally irrational. There's no evidence for the existence of God. Those who believe in God are therefore running away from reality, seeking consolation in a make-believe, fairy-tale world. Dawkins's statements about faith, whether drawn from *The God Delusion* or elsewhere, have become an integral part of the New Atheist critique of religion. Faith is "blind trust, in the absence of evidence, even in the teeth of evidence."[23] It's a "process of non-thinking" or "a persistently false belief held in the face of strong contradictory evidence."[24] It's "evil precisely because it requires no justification, and brooks no argument."[25]

Having debated Dawkins on several occasions, I've formed the impression that this last statement is of special importance to him. Since religion is irrational, it cannot defend its beliefs by an appeal to reason or science. It's therefore forced to *impose* them on people, especially by oppressive or violent means or by encouraging a culture of unquestioning obedience. There's a direct link in Dawkins's mind between faith and violence, and identifying this fixed idea helps us understand the inner logic of his criticism of religion.

Dawkins develops Harris's earlier argument for the irrationality of faith with much greater force and clarity. The irrationality of religious *beliefs*, he asserts, directly parallels the irrationality of religious *believers*, who are averse to offering any intellectual justification for their faith. Dawkins had been making this point for years before the events of 9/11, but the terrorist attacks gave a new plausibility to his argument. What sort of person would fly a plane into the side of a building? Only someone who was mad and evil.

For Dawkins, reason and science alike are to be celebrated because they emphasize the importance of beliefs being based on rational decisions, grounded in evidence. Dawkins sees no evidence for a God, so belief in God may be dismissed as irrational and unscientific. Science represents reason; religion represents superstition. The problems of the world are shaped by the great tension between the two, which will only disappear when superstition is eliminated. In other words, science and religion are locked in a battle to the death that science alone can win.

This neatly brings us to the second major theme in Dawkins's critique of religion: its propensity toward violence. Religion, Dawkins argues, has the capacity to incite otherwise innocent and peaceful people to violent thoughts and behavior, especially by deluding them into believing that they're serving God by their actions. (He rather glosses over Sam Harris's embarrassing fondness for "rational" violence.) Dawkins makes his point by an appeal to history, noting incidents such as the Crusades and the Spanish Inquisition that raise deep concerns about the potential of religion to engender violence and oppression. September 11 is simply the latest example in this catalog of acts of irrational violence.

I completely agree with Dawkins on two points here—first, that some such disgraceful episodes took place, and second, that some of them were caused by religion, either directly or indirectly. But is it really that simple? Let us turn for a moment to Michael Shermer, executive director of the Skeptics Society, which has as its motto the philosopher Spinoza's famous statement: "I have made a ceaseless effort not to ridicule, not to bewail, not to scorn human actions, but to understand them." Shermer rightly affirms that religion has been implicated in some dreadful human tragedies. But he doesn't stop there. He paints the full picture:

> However, for every one of these grand tragedies there are ten thousand acts of personal kindness and social good that go unreported. . . . Religion, like all social institutions of such historical depth and cultural impact, cannot be reduced to an unambiguous good or evil.[26]

Dawkins's reluctance to tell the full story seriously weakens the credibility of his argument. It's easy to argue that atheism is better than Christianity: you only need to ignore the good side of Christianity and the bad side of atheism, and Dawkins is rather good at both. But the inconvenient point is that nonreligious worldviews—such as Stalinism—can be just as oppressive as anything based on religious beliefs. We will return to this topic later, as it should be given proper weight in our discussion.

Dawkins's third line of criticism—the most interesting, in my view—relates to the natural sciences. Following the publication of his book *The Selfish Gene* (1976), he gained a well-deserved reputation as an outstanding popularizer of scientific ideas, especially those relating to evolutionary biology.[27] Although *The Selfish Gene* was critical of belief in God, Dawkins kept those criticisms on a fairly tight leash.[28] With the passage of time, however, the stridency of his criticisms increased, culminating in *The God Delusion*.

Bringing his scientific background, especially his interest in evolutionary biology, into play, Dawkins does more than argue that scientific belief *undermines* belief in God; he argues that it *explains it away* as an unintended outcome of human evolution. Believing in God is an "accidental by-product" of the evolutionary process. Religion arises from a "misfiring of something useful."[29]

It has always seemed to me that there's a problem here.[30] If Darwinian evolution is indeed a random process, how can we speak about "accidental" or "unintended" outcomes? Dawkins argues at several points in his books that the natural world may have the *appearance* of design, but this *appearance* of design or intentionality arises from random developments.[31] However, if Dawkins is right, surely *all* outcomes of the evolutionary process are "unintended." Or does he really think that evolution is guided by some kind of metaphorical mind that steers it in appropriate directions while permitting occasional digressions and byways?

The point Dawkins wants to make is that evolution did not intend that we should believe in God or be religious (two quite different notions). But Dawkins's earlier books, such as *The Blind Watchmaker* (1986), attest to the fact that he's deeply committed to the belief that *nothing* is intended.[32] *Everything* is accidental, even if it might look designed or seems to show other evidence of cosmic intentionality.

During the 1990s, to back up his notion that some people believe in God—when there's no God to believe in—because of evolutionary or cultural factors that secretly shape our thinking and guide it in this irrational direction, Dawkins popularized the belief that God was a "virus of the mind." This virus, he believed, spread through populations in much the same way as a disease.[33] Citing the example of Anthony

Kenny, a highly distinguished British philosopher who abandoned his Catholicism after thirty years, he wrote: "It must be a powerful infection indeed that took a man of his wisdom and intelligence—now President of the British Academy, no less—three decades to fight off." Religion is a "brilliantly successful virus" that contaminates even the best of minds.[34]

Though Dawkins's language about God as a "virus of the mind" was, I think, clearly intended to be *metaphorical*, some of his less sophisticated followers seem to take it literally. I recall speaking in a debate about atheism some years ago when, having delivered my piece and handed over to my opponent, I spotted a spare seat in the front row of the lecture hall. As I sat down, the woman next to me got to her feet, saying, "I don't want to catch your nasty God virus, thank you very much!"

This idea of God as a mental virus makes a halfhearted comeback in *The God Delusion*. But the dominant scientific explanation of the persistence of belief in God in this volume is that of the meme.[35] Dawkins invented this notion back in 1976, arguing that there was a fundamental analogy between the transmission of genetic information and cultural information. He coined the term *meme* to refer to a hypothetical unit of imitation or replication, by which ideas—above all, the idea of God—could be transmitted within a culture. Memes infect people's brains, Dawkins tells us, just like a virus.[36]

But what's the scientific evidence for the meme? And if

there's a "God meme" that inclines people toward believing in God, is there also a "no-God meme" that inclines people toward atheism? Do memes transmit *ideas* (such as belief in God) or *behavioral patterns* (such as religiosity)?[37] And since there's no evidence for memes, does that mean that there is a meme that causes us to believe in memes?

In a sense, the debate is now over. The meme is now widely regarded as little more than a biological fiction. Its death as a serious hypothesis can probably be dated to 2005, when the *Journal of Memetics*, launched in 1997 (arguably at the height of interest in the idea), ceased publication. Its last issue contained what amounted to an obituary from one of the concept's more thoughtful critics. "Memetics," he wrote, "has been a short-lived fad whose effect has been to obscure more than it has been to enlighten. I am afraid that . . . as an identifiable discipline, [it] will not be widely missed."[38] God seems to have outlived the meme, which some envisioned as God's ultimate nemesis.

Finally, Dawkins argues that atheism is simpler and more elegant than belief in God. This is certainly debatable. Earlier we noted Dawkins's approving reference to the influential and respected philosopher Anthony Kenny. A casual reader might assume that Kenny became an atheist when he abandoned his Catholicism. In fact, he became an agnostic. For Kenny, the God question cannot be settled conclusively by the evidence at our disposal. He argues, with characteristic philosophical rigor, that atheism is obliged to make a much stronger claim than theism:

> Many different definitions may be offered of the word "God." Given this fact, atheism makes a much stronger claim than theism does. The atheist says that no matter what definition you choose, "God exists" is always false. The theist only claims that there is some definition which will make "God exists" true. . . . A claim to knowledge needs to be substantiated; ignorance need only be confessed.[39]

Readers of *The God Delusion* will realize immediately that this clearly contradicts Dawkins's assertions both of the simplicity of atheism in relation to belief in God, and of the intellectual and moral deficiencies of agnosticism when compared to atheism. But more on that later. For now, let us move on to the third of our quartet of writers.

DANIEL DENNETT

The American philosopher Daniel Dennett (born 1942) is noted for his interest in exploring the broader cultural implications to human society of Darwin's theory of evolution. In *Darwin's Dangerous Idea* (1995), he developed the idea that belief in God can be explained away on evolutionary grounds.[40] He took this approach further in *Breaking the Spell* (2006), arguing that natural selection has programmed us to believe in God when there's really no God to believe in.[41] Dennett does not focus on the alleged irrationality or immorality of faith in this volume (although on such matters he clearly shares the opinions of his colleagues within the New Atheism), and his relative lack of verbal aggressiveness and ridicule possibly explains why *Breaking the Spell* failed to sell as well as other leading works of the movement.

Given the importance of the notion of religion to the New Atheist writers, it is clearly essential to have a workable definition. If you're going to criticize something, you need to be able to say what it is. So what does Dennett suggest in *Breaking the Spell*? He declares that "a religion without God or gods is like a vertebrate without a backbone."[42] I have to say that if I were leading a high school discussion about the nature of religion, this would certainly be the first definition we'd consider. It would also certainly be the first we'd have to reject! It is simply inadequate. Vertebrates, by definition, have backbones, but following a religion does not necessarily mean worshipping God or gods. There are, after all, nontheistic religions, such as most forms of Buddhism. So why does Dennett choose this unworkable definition? The answer seems to be that he wants to explain belief in God in terms of evolutionary theory. To believe in God, he asserts, is a fantasy that once carried some kind of survival advantages. But religion simply cannot be equated with belief in God, no matter how convenient this might be for Dennett's polemical agendas.

Dennett is a professional philosopher. One of the great strengths of *Breaking the Spell* could have been a robust philosophical critique of arguments for belief in God. I was expecting to find a state-of-the-art defense of atheism, paralleling the powerful defenses of theism offered recently by leading theistic philosophers such as Richard Swinburne and William Lane Craig. Yet where we might have expected a philosophical feast, we're merely thrown a few stale crumbs. Dennett offers us just six pages of reflection on whether there might actually be any good reasons for believing in God.[43] His approach here is quirky, to say the least:

> I will just give a brief bird's eye view of the domain of inquiry, expressing my own verdicts but not the reasoning that has gone into them, and providing references to a few pieces that may not be familiar to many.[44]

After reading Dennett's sparse analysis, I felt a paraphrase of this sentence would make its significance somewhat clearer:

22

I will just give a quick summary of my own view of things, which is so obviously right that it doesn't really need to be supported by reason or evidence, and refer to my own earlier writings that some people inexplicably seem not to have read.

These are not the best six pages in the book. Dennett offers little more than a précis of an introductory and somewhat impressionistic lecture on the philosophy of religion, which gives only the case for the prosecution of God, not the defense. In fact, the most detailed New Atheist engagement with traditional philosophical arguments for the existence of God is found in Dawkins's *The God Delusion*. Neither Dawkins's grasp of those arguments nor his attempted rebuttals carry much weight.[45]

Dennett's baffling disinclination to engage properly and rigorously has seriously impoverished the New Atheism at this critically important point. I must confess that I came away from reading *Breaking the Spell* with a deep sense of frustration and dissatisfaction.

Another curious feature of the book is its excessive dependency upon Dawkins's notion of the meme, an idea already falling out of favor as Dennett was writing. Dawkins and Dennett clearly understand the meme in different ways, which is only what you'd expect given that the meme is clearly something imagined rather than observed. While Dawkins believes that the dynamics of religious memes mean that their effect is always to corrupt, Dennett's take is that "belief in belief"—that is, a desire to believe, or a sense that belief is basically good—is one of the most effective techniques for religious memes to render themselves immune to the antibodies of doubt or critical reason. A critic might not unreasonably wonder what the evidence for this bold assertion could be.

But Dennett has already rushed on to other things. He suggests that, just as human beings have evolved a receptor system for sweet things, so in a similar way we may have evolved some kind of "god center" in our brains. Such a center might depend on a "mystical gene" that was favored by natural selection because people with it tend to survive better.[46]

It's an interesting idea and well worth exploring. After all, Christianity has always argued that we have a "soft spot" or "homing instinct" for God. That's why God just won't go away! Dennett might help clarify how this works, but what scientific evidence does he advance for this mystical gene? Unfortunately we find only mights and maybes, speculations and suppositions rather than the rigorous evidence-driven and evidence-based arguments regarded as normal for the natural sciences. For example, we're told (I quote from the gushing jacket blurb) that "ideas could have spread from individual superstitions via shamanism and the early 'wild' strains of religion." Perhaps it's not surprising that Dennett's theories have been so heavily criticized by his peers as being evidence-free and tentative beliefs, unconvincingly passed off as the cutting edge of scientific research.

Dennett argues that it is necessary to call on "the best minds on the planet" to study religion, such is its importance for humanity. I entirely agree with this general principle, but just who are these best minds? Dennett dismisses scholars of religion as "second-rate" thinkers,[47] and he seems to find it obvious that religion should only be studied and evaluated by those whose minds are unclouded by any religious commitments. The people he appears to have in mind are, as the sociologist Tina Beattie recently observed, "a highly unsympathetic Western elite," more concerned to "destroy those beliefs" than to understand them.[48]

To sum up, Dennett presents himself in *Breaking the Spell* as a bold intellectual trailblazer offering evidence and arguments that will destroy faith. In fact, it's the patience, not the faith of its readers, that's challenged by Dennett's tedious analysis. This disappointing book, which tends to be cited far less frequently than the remaining canonical writings of the New Atheism, shows Dennett the philosopher struggling to make sense of a scientific field he does not really seem to understand, offering speculative theories that could conceivably impress the ignorant and impressionable but leave everyone else struggling to reconcile the gross disparity between what was promised and what's actually delivered. If only he'd focused on the philosophical debate instead of allowing himself to be locked into pseudoscientific babble about memes! Then the New Atheism would have had the significant philosophical foundation it presently lacks.

If Dennett comes across as being a little dull, no one could ever make that accusation against our fourth New Atheist writer. It's time to turn to the master of the well-turned phrase and well-placed verbal stiletto, Anglo-American journalist Christopher Hitchens (born 1949).

Christopher Hitchens

Hitchens's *God Is Not Great* (2007) is by far the most entertaining of the New Atheist works. It's driven by a passionate anger about religion, unquestionably fueled in part by the events of 9/11. But it reveals a deeper anxiety, which I believe underlies the work of other New Atheist writers as well—namely the obstinate refusal of religion to die out as predicted by secular theorists since the 1960s. God just won't go away. Hitchens's alarmist rhetoric appeals to a subconscious fear within the West's liberal intellectual elite. We are losing the battle for social dominance! Religion is resurgent! Atheists and skeptics are in mortal danger! As Hitchens ominously warns his readers in one of his most outspoken (and characteristically unsubstantiated) pronouncements: "People of faith are in their different ways planning your and my destruction."[49] To

Hitchens's devotees, this is what 9/11 is all about. We must resist religion before it wreaks further havoc upon us.

God Is Not Great is a remarkable piece of theater, characterized by its quick-fire aphorisms and finely honed insults. Hitchens uses the brightest colors in his palette and his broadest brushstrokes to paint a vivid picture of religion as dysfunctional, depraved, and decadent. Written in some haste (four months),[50] the book shows what some might uncharitably see as obvious signs of inconsistency and lack of evidential and argumentative integrity. But nobody can doubt Hitchens's commitment to his beliefs or deny his skill as a wordsmith.

He has a wonderful ear for a good phrase—such as "religion poisons everything." Even more strikingly (as we've already noted), "religion kills."[51] The faults of the world are to be laid at the door of primitive superstitions that hold us back from our rational and scientific destiny. Eliminate religion, which has led only to violence, intellectual dishonesty, oppression, and social division, and the world will be a better place.

God Is Not Great is written with such conviction and confidence that if self-assurance alone were an indication of truth, Hitchens would win his arguments hands down. He has a marvelous way of persuading his readers that his analysis of some core religious ideas is skimpy on account of their intrinsic irrationality, rather than any inability on his part to handle them properly. For example, the chapter boldly entitled "The

Metaphysical Claims of Religion Are False" skims the surface of a potentially interesting debate, leaving us unsure what those metaphysical claims might be or what's wrong with them. But at least we come away knowing that Hitchens thinks they're merely so much donkey poo along the road of life.

It's not exactly an argument, is it?

I've often discussed Hitchens's oracular writing style with his more enthusiastic supporters, who tend to take the line that he's such a genius that he does not need to waste his time exploring religious ideas in depth. He's declared that they're ridiculous, and that's good enough for them. The conclusion is what matters; there is no need to explain how it was reached. But is it rational to treat Hitchens as some kind of guru, to trust the person rather than the arguments or evidence? I wonder if some of his devotees, having stopped believing in God, find they simply have to trust and worship someone else.[52] To return to these metaphysical claims we mentioned above, it seems to me they have not been properly engaged, let alone damaged, by Hitchens. But his devotees won't have this. Hitchens has spoken, and the matter is settled.

Another interesting feature of *God Is Not Great* is the way Hitchens cherry-picks historical anecdotes to make his case. His use of historical evidence is shaped by the controlling story (often referred to as a "metanarrative") that is a characteristic feature of the New Atheism—above all, the idea that those who entertain religious belief are deluded and hence potentially dangerous to society at large. I found myself wondering why Hitchens's appeal to history is so selective and self-serving. Doesn't he realize that his opponents could use exactly the same technique to make the opposite point?

Let us look at one of the anecdotes Hitchens weaves into his account of the irrational and immoral idiocy of religious thinkers. The Christian writer Timothy Dwight (1752–1811), who was president of Yale College, Connecticut (later to become Yale University), opposed smallpox vaccination. For Hitchens, this is typical of religious people. They're backward-looking fools, and Dwight's ridiculous position just shows how religious obscurantism stood in the way of scientific advance then, as it continues to now. Religion poisons all attempts at human progress. The specific example confirms the general principle.

Well, Dwight did indeed oppose smallpox vaccination. But Hitchens forgets to mention (if he knew at all) that a president of Princeton, Jonathan Edwards—now widely regarded as America's greatest religious thinker—had died a few decades earlier in 1758 after receiving the vaccine. As a strong supporter of scientific advance, Edwards was committed to this new medical procedure and wanted to demonstrate to his students that it was safe.[53] Might not his advocation of smallpox vaccination been mentioned in Hitchens's narrative? After all, it unfortunately cost Edwards his life. Yet any such admission would force Hitchens to make some rhetorically damaging qualifications in his analysis—such as "only some" religious thinkers oppose scientific advance. His superimposition of a New Atheist template on history leads to the filtering out of highly important evidential inconveniences and inconsistencies. Does his intended readership expect—or even depend on—such highly prejudiced history to sustain their polemic against religion?

To explore just how persuasive this method can be, let us amuse ourselves for a moment by imitating Hitchens's disregard for historical accuracy and presenting a piece of historical analysis that's a perfect, if theistically inverted, image of Hitchens's approach in *God Is Not Great*.

The great atheist writer George Bernard Shaw (1856–1950) opposed smallpox vaccination in the 1930s, ridiculing it as a "delusion." He dismissed leading scientists whose work was cited in support of it—such as Louis Pasteur and Joseph Lister—as charlatans who knew nothing about the scientific method. If I were to use Hitchens's cherry-picking approach to history, I could argue that this outrageous antiscientific attitude on the part of this leading atheist just shows that atheism is dogmatic and hidebound, unwilling to take scientific advance seriously. All right-thinking people will thus reject atheism as outmoded and reactionary. Except that it isn't that simple—is it? Nobody of any intelligence or integrity could be satisfied with such a manipulative and flagrantly biased attitude to history—could they?

We see the same extraordinary bias in Hitchens's perplexing discussion of two leading Christian activists—Dietrich Bonhoeffer (1906–45) and Martin Luther King Jr. (1929–68)—whose moral and spiritual examples in the face of oppression have had a deep impact on Western culture. Hitchens boldly declares, without the slightest interest in historical reality, that Bonhoeffer's readiness to face death in his opposition to Hitler's Nazism was based on an "admirable but nebulous humanism."[54] Bonhoeffer's letters and papers from prison as he awaited execution give a completely different perspective, focused as they are on the crucifixion of Christ as an inspiration and example in times of great distress. But Hitchens doesn't want that story to be told.

Again, Hitchens tells us that the American civil-rights leader Martin Luther King Jr. was not a Christian in any real sense of the word.[55] There's no evidence for this bold assertion, only the need to have reality fitting neatly into Hitchens's dogmatic mold. Hitchens's argument here, which is never explicitly stated, seems to go like this:

Major premise: religion is evil and violent.
Minor premise: Dietrich Bonhoeffer and Martin Luther King Jr. were good people.
Conclusion: Bonhoeffer and King were not really religious.

After debating Hitchens in Washington, I formed an impression that has remained with me ever since. I like him. He is great with words (if possibly not quite so hot on facts) and has a tremendous sense of humor and a scathing wit, which makes other New Atheist writers sound dull and wearisome in comparison. He's a straight talker, and I have no doubt that he genuinely believes religion is evil. I still think he's wrong on some core questions, as the rest of this book will indicate. But he's such a stimulating writer that his ideas invite further debate. It was with great sadness that I learned recently that Hitchens has been diagnosed with cancer of the esophagus. I hope he will not mind that I—along with many others—am remembering him in my prayers.

In this chapter, we've looked at the leading representatives of the New Atheism and glanced briefly at their anxieties and approaches. In the second and third parts of the book, we'll explore the themes that have emerged. But let us first consider how the New Atheism differs from other forms of atheism.

2

WHAT'S "NEW" ABOUT
THE NEW ATHEISM?

At first sight, the New Atheism might seem little more than a movement demanding equal rights and responsibilities for atheists, like the civil rights movement of the 1960s or the more recent movement for gay rights. But journalist Gary Wolf, though clearly sympathetic to the agenda of the New Atheism, points out that the analogy with such pressure groups is seriously flawed.

> Gay politics is strictly civil rights: Live and let live. But the atheist movement, by [Dawkins's] lights, has no choice but to aggressively spread the good news. Evangelism is a moral imperative. Dawkins does not merely disagree with religious myths. He disagrees with tolerating them.[1]

Wolf's analysis casts light on why so many moderate atheists seem to find the New Atheism something of an embarrassment. It paints them as judgmental, dogmatic, and fanatical, aggressively seeking to expand their cultural space rather than encourage an ethos of mutual toleration. The American civil rights movement did not ridicule whites or demand they be excluded from public office: it campaigned for equal acceptance for all.

We'll return to this point shortly, but it may first be useful to examine how the "New" Atheism differs from "older" forms.[2]

THE NEW ATHEISM AS ANTI-THEISM

Atheism comes in different forms. We are probably all familiar with the atheism that entails neither hostility toward God nor even an active belief that God does not exist. This "apathetic atheism" or "atheism of indifference" is probably more accurately described as a form of agnosticism. There's a world of difference between "not believing that God exists" and "believing that God does not exist."

Then there's the atheism whose followers, having given serious consideration to the issues, *do* actively believe that God does not exist. While apathetic atheism offers (and needs to offer) little or no rational justification for its position, what I think is best called "committed" atheism (though others prefer "skeptical" or "positive" atheism) represents a definite stance, based on certain quite explicit arguments and concerns. Sociological research suggests that there are probably fewer committed atheists than apathetic ones.

Committed atheists hold to a surprisingly wide range of positions. Some reject God but decline to place their faith in anything else (such as human reason, scientific progress, or nontheistic spiritualities). Others maintain that rejection of God leads to an unacceptable spiritual aridity and therefore supplement this deficiency through an appeal to nontheistic Eastern mysticisms or spiritualities. Others insist that rejection of God does not entail abandoning the notion of transcendence and believe that it is meaningful to continue to speak of transcendent ideas such as "goodness."

Neither apathetic atheism nor committed atheism is necessarily or characteristically anti-theistic. Adherents of these forms generally see them as positive movements and often display a deep concern for ethics and spirituality. They think that those who believe in God are wrong, but they have no particular animosity against them or their ideas. Having little hostility toward religious belief or practice, they're often happy to engage in constructive dialogue and debate with those who do believe in God. (An excellent example is the recent informed and stimulating discussion between

35

two leading Italian thinkers, the atheist Umberto Eco and Cardinal Carlo Maria Martini.[3])

The New Atheism is different. It's defined not so much by being white, male, and middle class—though it is worth noting that its four leading representatives are all Anglo-Saxon Protestant males from remarkably similar backgrounds of privilege and power[4]—as by its anti-theism—an intense anger against religion, which is held to poison everything. Christopher Hitchens puts it with a commendable concision: "I am not even an atheist so much as I am an antitheist."[5] This anti-theism is equally evident in the writings of the other "Four Horsemen." But surely this leads to the group defining itself by what it's against rather than what it's for.

If so, would it be fair to conclude that the New Atheism is dependent on its enemies for its core identity? Greg Epstein, the humanist chaplain to Harvard University, certainly thinks so.

While atheism is the lack of belief in any god, anti-theism means actively seeking out the worst aspects of faith in god and portraying them as representative of all religion. Anti-theism seeks to shame and embarrass people away from religion, browbeating them about the stupidity of belief in a bellicose god.[6]

Epstein suggests that it might be a good idea if anti-theists were to focus on doing some good things themselves rather than repetitively lampooning religion by discriminatory stereotyping.

Epstein's criticism of the New Atheism resonates with the concerns of many humanists and atheists who are shocked by its extremism and overstatement and alarmed at its ridicule of saints as villains and fools. Christopher Hitchens recently slammed Mother Teresa, declaring her "a fanatic and a fundamentalist and a fraud," arguing that "millions of people are much worse off because of her life." It was a shame, he declared, that there was no hell for her to go to. It was a foolish move, and Hitchens later generously apologized for it.[7] (One of Hitchens's former colleagues drolly commented, "My sympathies were with Mother Teresa. If you were sitting in rags in a gutter in Calcutta, who would be more likely to give you a bowl of soup?"[8])

The New Atheists, like other committed atheists, believe that there is no God. Yet whereas other atheists see this as their *primary* belief and focus, the New Atheism makes it *secondary* to its all-out, undiluted, and unqualified opposition to any form of religious belief and practice. There's actually little evidence that "religion," considered generically, is as weird or as dangerous as the New Atheism would have us believe, but that's not the point. This way of thinking has a deep appeal to some religiously alienated individuals because it offers them at least the semblance of intellectual depth and moral principle.

On several occasions I've been earnestly told by New Atheist foot soldiers that I have no business being a professor in a leading British university. After all, they inform me, I believe in God and am therefore stupid, evil, and mentally instable. I ought to be locked up for the public good. When I'm openly abused in this way, I find my most vociferous defenders are moderate atheists—often academics—who are sickened by such mindless hostility and alarmed at the damage it's inflicting on the public image of atheism. Polite society and academic culture make a proper distinction between people and their ideas, believing that it's possible to debate ideas without debasing the people who hold them. But the New Atheism seems to be out to ridicule both.

The Wider New Atheism: The Online Communities

In chapter 1, I pointed out that the New Atheism cannot be defined or described simply in terms of the canonical writings of the "Four Horsemen." It's generated a global community of individuals who find these authors authoritative and inspirational guides to the rational and scientific worldview they believe holds the key to the future of the human race. The Web communities and blogs that have come into being provide what sociologist Peter Berger calls "plausibility structures" for the New Atheism[9]—above all, a sense of shared identity and solidarity, especially in the face of perceived external and internal threats.

I've been studying these Web sites and virtual communities since late 2004 and find they give a fascinating insight into how New Atheist ideas are understood and received at a broader level. Every student of theology will be aware of the massive gap between academic theory and religious belief and practice. A similar fissure exists within the New Atheism, which offers rich pickings for academic sociologists in the future. The popular expressions of the movement often differ significantly, both in terms of intellectual content and degree of fanaticism, from the core ideas of its leaders. These blogs and online communities seem to me to be the heartbeat of the New Atheism and should be given full weight by both its critics and supporters.

As we'll see later in this chapter, the New Atheism has a surprisingly small footprint in terms of physical meetings and communities (the contrast with Christian churches being particularly obvious and significant at this point). Yet the online presence of the movement is much greater. By February 2010, the forum hosted by the Richard Dawkins Foundation for Reason and Science[10]—which seems to exist to promote Richard Dawkins and atheism in that order—had attracted eighty-five thousand members globally and achieved the status of being the world's largest atheist online community.

As might be expected, these online atheist forums are characterized by a gut aversion to religion, which is regularly condemned as irrational and immoral. Even allowing that the anonymity of blogging can encourage a ferocity of expression untamed by normal social conventions and restraints, the stridency displayed by these militant atheists often seems bizarre to outsiders, whether religious or not. Religion, it is declared, is like Nazism and needs to be eliminated, not understood. Respecting religion is like admiring Hitler—morally unacceptable and strategically inept. While those who are outside the New Atheist bubble will probably think this is simply paranoid nonsense, many of its bloggers are convinced that religion is out to get them. A preemptive strike is necessary. The best form of defense is attack. Kill them before they kill you.

NEW ATHEIST ANXIETIES

Yet I've noticed recently that all is not well within these virtual communities. They had an upbeat feel in the heady days of 2006 and 2007 when the New Atheism seemed to be like a bright new sun dawning on the world. But not now. Is a "crisis of faith" beginning to emerge?

A small example may illustrate one of the crystallizing points of concern. The large sales figures of the published writings of the "Four Horsemen" were seen by many secularist commentators as a surefire indication that atheism was displacing religion in the public domain. These figures marked a cultural watershed. Or did they? Certainly Dawkins's *The God Delusion* became a best seller, selling nearly a million copies in North America.[11] But Rick Warren's Christian book *The Purpose Driven Life* is reliably reported as having sold nearly thirty million copies in the same sales area since its publication in 2002. If the New Atheism's flagship book could muster only around 3 percent of the sales of a religious best seller such as Warren's (which attracted considerably less media attention), what does that say about the numerical strength and cultural influence of the New Atheism?

In fact, a survey of religious beliefs in the United States undertaken at Baylor University in late 2007—after the peak in interest in the New Atheism following the publication of its core manifestos—revealed that only 4 percent of Americans explicitly define themselves as atheists.[12] The comparative sales of Dawkins and Warren thus fairly accurately reflect the relative sizes of the religious and atheist communities in the United States.

Interestingly, 11 percent of the national sample reported that they had "no religion." Atheist Web sites tend to put a spin on this figure, making out it refers to people who do not believe in God and so is therefore indicative of the growing influence of atheism. But while 4 percent of the American population do indeed self-define as atheists according to this survey, the remaining 7 percent appear to be merely "unchurched" rather than "irreligious."[13] American church planters have long realized that there are many Americans with religious inclinations and interests who have simply not connected with the institution of the church.[14]

The failure of the core writings of the New Atheism to achieve big sales has been the topic of much anxiety on atheist blogs. Why does Warren's book sell so many more copies than Dawkins's? New Atheist bloggers would rather ridicule Warren than reflect on his significance, as this revealing but perhaps not particularly wise comment makes clear: "Richard Dawkins has one advantage over Rick Warren. All of his books were purchased by people who can read. And actually read books."[15] Such remarks seem to reinforce the growing public perception that the New Atheism has become arrogant and increasingly disconnected from the real world.

The big concern, which began to emerge in 2007 as reviewers tried to work out the possible long-term significance of the movement, was that the New Atheism might turn out to be a fad—a short-lived cultural phenomenon. What exactly was new about it? What insights and facts did it introduce to existing debates? Bruce DeSilva of the Associated Press seemed to capture the consensus on this matter. Commenting on *God Is Not Great*, he remarked, "Hitchens has nothing new to say, although it must be acknowledged that he says it exceptionally well."[16] The New Atheism certainly had a novelty value—but this lay in the intensity of its ridicule of religion, not the substance of its criticisms.

Other doubts about the orthodoxy of the New Atheism regularly emerge on some atheist Web sites. Sam Harris's ruthless portrayal of religion as intrinsically and monolithically evil is seen as especially troubling. Is it really that straightforward? Can you persuade ordinary people to believe such stuff? Anxiety about this point bubbles up on several Web sites open to more critical reflection, those on which intrepid souls dare to challenge the prevailing tub-thumping. Dark talk about the exaggeration of evidence is becoming increasingly common.

But the most intense anger on these forums is directed against atheists who are seen to be accommodating toward people of faith or who otherwise seem to betray the high ideals and core dogmas of the New Atheism. These are the traitors, the collaborators, the quislings who contaminate the movement, infecting it with a moderation that hinders its elimination of religion.

To illustrate this point, let us consider the reaction on New Atheist blogs to a representative of the older, more reflective form of atheism—the mild-mannered British writer Julian Baggini (born 1968), author of the eminently readable *A Very Short Introduction to Atheism*.[17] I had the pleasure of debating issues of faith with Baggini some years ago and found him intelligent and respectful—the sort of person who could give atheism a good name. That's what makes the events of 2009 so intriguing.

THE INTERESTING CASE OF JULIAN BAGGINI

Early in that year, Baggini published an article in the Norwegian humanist magazine *Fri Tanke* (Free Thought).[18] The magazine helpfully reproduced the original English version on its Web site, with a headline—not chosen by Baggini himself—that was like a red rag to a bull: "The New Atheist Movement Is Destructive."[19] The response within the New Atheist online community was immediate and aggressive, apparently based more on the title than the substance of the article. Baggini later reflected ruefully on the reaction to his piece. "I have been burned as a heretic by many of the commenters at

RichardDawkins.net, who call me variously a flea, a fool, and a pompous air bag."[20] They called him quite a few other things as well, but they can't be published here.

So what did Baggini actually say? What outrageous statements elicited such a furious reaction? As a seasoned observer of certain New Atheist Web sites, I've learned their ground rules: the degree of ridicule heaped upon a given viewpoint is a measure of the degree of threat it poses to the core beliefs of the online community. With a certain dreary inevitability, the movement's bloggers assume that anyone who dares to criticize the New Atheism automatically exposes himself as irrational, antiscientific, and a secret supporter of religion—in a word, a traitor. Yet Baggini had merely made two points that most outside observers of the New Atheism regard as representing significant and valid criticisms of the movement.

First, he pointed out that the New Atheism is characterized more by its attacks on religion than by its own positive beliefs—as, for example, in Dawkins's unqualified assertion that "there is a logical path from religious faith to evil deeds." For Baggini, this simply reinforces the adage that "an atheist without a bishop to bash is like a fish without water." In fact, he argues, it is worse than that. It just reinforces the widespread suspicion that many atheists "need an enemy to give them their identity." A trawl of leading atheist Web sites amply confirms Baggini's fears. Many New Atheist foot soldiers see themselves as engaged in a crusade to rid the world of religion. This holy war is their reason for living, the center of their existence.

Second, Baggini complained that the New Atheism arrogantly claims to have a monopoly on reason. "With its talk of 'spells' and 'delusions,' it gives the impression that only through stupidity or crass disregard for reason could anyone be anything other than an atheist."[21] It's essential to recognize the limits of reason, Baggini argued, and to accept that reason and evidence play a significant role in religious belief.[22] Dawkins's crude definition of faith as a "cop-out" or an "excuse to evade the need to think and evaluate evidence" was simply "arrogant, and attributes to reason a power it does not have."

Shouldn't the New Atheists be a little more skeptical about reason? Baggini wondered. Dawkins and others simply reinforce the unhelpful stereotype that atheists are "men who look only to science for answers, are dismissive of religion and over-confident in their own rightness." The New Atheism is characterized by a dogmatism that permits neither doubt nor respect for disagreement.

Now, this may be heresy to some in the New Atheism, but it is the mainstream response from many of those who are philosophically and scientifically informed—something to which we'll return later. Baggini is simply telling things the way they are. The reaction he received is hardly commensurate with a community that claims to cherish reason and evidence—even when they subvert its own beliefs.

The Strange Story of the Dawkins Forum

The defensive-aggressiveness within the New Atheist community is perhaps seen at its clearest and most destructive in a recent ferocious controversy over the shutdown of the Dawkins Forum. By early 2010, this section of the Web site of the Richard Dawkins Foundation for Reason and Science was firmly established as the leading atheist virtual community. Then many of its members found that they were locked out, unable to post comments.

The shutdown began on February 23, 2010, when a decision was made to close the existing forum section of the Web site to allow for greater editorial control. It remains unclear precisely who was behind this decision, but the announcement took activists by surprise and caused immediate fury. Peter Harrison, one of its moderators, was shocked to learn that his role had been terminated. The news that the "world's busiest atheist forum" was being shut down, he fulminated, was a matter of "lies, censorship and cowardice."[23] He and others had been viciously betrayed by their colleagues at RichardDawkins.net.

Other members were not slow to express their outrage, many using scatological and hate-charged language that simply cannot be repeated here. Bloggers swamped other freethinking sites on the Web with an extraordinary outpouring of resentment, anger, bile, and scarcely concealed contempt for those seen to be responsible for this decision—including Josh Timonen, who managed the Web site, and Richard Dawkins himself.

Dawkins, then on a lecture tour of Australia, was clearly taken aback by this unexpected turn of events. He responded on February 24 in a hastily written posting, entitled "Outrage," that criticized the "ludicrously hyperbolic animosity" that the decision had provoked. He expressed the sadness that any "greatly liked and respected person" (does he mean himself?) would experience if he or she were "subjected to personal vilification on an unprecedented scale, from anonymous commentors."[24] Dawkins was clearly distressed at being called a "suppurating rat's rectum"—to mention only one of the choice descriptions alleged to be used by the rebellious members of this suppressed oasis of rationality and science.

Let us be clear: Dawkins was clearly treated unfairly by his many New Atheist critics. A Nietzschean "herd mentality" displaced any pretense at valuing cool and clinical judgments of reason, and he was its unfortunate target. He has my total sympathy. As Baggini rightly pointed out, many New Atheist fanatics derive their identity from identifying and vilifying their enemies. In this remarkable turnabout, Dawkins came to be seen as such an enemy. The ranks of the godless faithful closed against him.

Many atheist bloggers despaired of the impact that closing the forum would have on the public reputation of the New Atheism. How long, one of them wondered, before this was used as evidence that atheists cannot form healthy communities, or became an anti-Dawkins talking point in "good without god" debates?[25] In fact, the suppression of the forum—though an obvious embarrassment for the New Atheism, not least because it deflated some of the more pompous overstatements of its communal virtues—was not the real problem. The big concern was the very public nature of this civil war, which drew aside a curtain and allowed outsiders to peer inside the citadel. They did not much like what they saw. Instead of being treated to a "feast of reason and flow of the soul,"[26] they found prejudice, a profound lack of intellectual ability or inquisitiveness, and an instinctive contempt for those who disagreed with the New Atheism.

Again, let us be clear that Dawkins was absolutely right to call time on some of the contributors to his forum, particularly those whose sick comments suggested that they might be social psychopaths or otherwise mentally disturbed. I'm not easily shocked, but in the past I've found myself disturbed by the simplistic sloganeering, venomous contempt, rhetorical violence, and sheer hate directed by some of these bloggers against religion. Nobody does nasty as well as New Atheist Web sites. As Dawkins himself noted, this unpleasant characteristic was doubtless encouraged by the lack of accountability ensured by anonymous postings.[27] Yet isn't such irrational hatred what the New Atheists want us to believe is characteristic only of *religion*?

But the story doesn't end there. Dawkins dedicated his 2009 book, *The Greatest Show on Earth*, to his young disciple, Josh Timonen, who ran the Dawkins Web site. In October 2010, Dawkins filed a lawsuit against this same Timonen, alleging that he'd defrauded Dawkins of hundreds of thousands of dollars raised by marketing atheist merchandise and Dawkins memorabilia through the Web site.[28] Modestly describing himself as "the world's best known and most respected atheist" (a judgment that very few atheists I know would affirm), Dawkins demanded $950,000 in damages. Timonen responded by speaking of his "ultimate betrayal" and a "baseless vendetta" against him.[29] This very public scandal does nothing to help the public image of the New Atheism. We're used to hearing about financial scandals in religious organizations, but this one was meant to be above that sort of thing.

No wonder so many now think the New Atheism is

looking more and more like another New Religious Movement. However, to use the categories of the sociology of religion, it behaves like a sect rather than a church. It has its boundaries, which are rigorously policed and enforced within the community. It has its own infallible texts and demands that its leading figures be treated with a respect and reverence that it conspicuously fails to apply to everyone else.

I, along with others, prefer to regard it more like a form of celebrity culture.[30] Certainly a fixation on celebrity would explain why the New Atheism is so obsessed with the sales figures of its core texts and so irritated by those who criticize Dawkins and his colleagues. (To include the name of any of the "Four Horsemen" in a book title—as I did with *The Dawkins Delusion?*[31]—is regarded as unspeakably arrogant by New Atheist devotees. How dare anyone name-drop such an intergalactically significant individual? Obviously they hope to be sprinkled with some stardust as a result!) Worried atheists outside the New Atheist bubble are alarmed that personality cults are overtaking this new movement and that followers are being encouraged simply to echo the views and actions of their gurus. (The secularist group called Freethinkers, which is "guided by reason and logic," has on sale a T-shirt printed with advice on how to tackle life's great ethical questions. Just ask, "What would Dawkins do?"[32]) The following comment reflects one concerned atheist's alarm at the uncritical adulation meted out to the "Four Horsemen" by some New Atheist Web sites:

> As much as I tend to agree with the neo-atheists phil-osophically, I worry a bit about the quasi-evangelical fervor of many of their "followers." Old tendencies die hard (if at all), and I think many of those who've abandoned monotheistic religions for atheism are still inclined to treat their intellectual heroes like cult figures. I suppose this could be the inevitable first stage of any transformation of values, but the herd instinct in action always sends a shiver down my spine.[33]

When the *Independent*—widely regarded as the most secu-larist British newspaper—voted Dawkins one of the smuggest people in Britain in 2009, one atheist blogger responded with obvious exasperation at the implied critique of Dawkins's infallibility: "Richard Dawkins is not even vaguley [*sic*] smug—he is just RIGHT. He is also highly intelligent."[34]

There's an important motif embedded in this statement. New Atheists are clever. They're smart enough to break free from the delusions and false assurances of religion. In short: they're "Bright"—with a capital *B*. This brings us to another important development in the New Atheist world.

THE INVENTION OF THE "BRIGHT"

Realizing that the term *atheist* was unspeakably dull and loaded with unhelpful and generally negative associations, two Californian educationalists—Paul Geisert and Mynga Futrell—invented the term *Brights* to designate those with naturalistic worldviews. Just as *gays* was adopted as a more upbeat way to designate homosexuals, *Brights* was coined as a positive term for atheists and their fellow travelers.

Geisert and Futrell launched their rebranding campaign at an atheist conference in Florida in spring 2003. It gained immediate support from Richard Dawkins and Daniel Dennett, both of whom promoted its agendas in leading British and American liberal-leaning newspapers.[35] Dawkins's advocacy in the UK proved especially successful, and many in the media believed that a new force was emerging in Western culture—"the future looks Bright."

Let us explore this fascinating development a little further. When commenting in 2006 on the rise of the Brights in the UK, journalist Gary Wolf noted that the Brights' meetup—this term is used in preference to "meeting"—in London was one of the largest and best organized nationwide.[36] Thanks to its excellent Web site, the topics and dates of these meetups, some of which were held jointly with London Atheists, are available in the public domain.[37] Table 1 sets out this basic

information from the first meetup of September 2003 to the
most recent.

Table 1
London Brights Meetups, 2003–10

Date	Attendance	Date	Attendance	Date	Attendance
Sept. 2003	13	Jan. 2005	15	May 2006	4
Oct. 2003	Canceled	Feb. 2005	20	June 2006	7
Nov. 2003	17	Mar. 2005	19	July 2006	30
Dec. 2003	17	Apr. 2005	19	Sept. 2006	33
Jan. 2004	Canceled	May 2005	15	Sept. 2006	24
Feb. 2004	Canceled	June 2005	16	Oct. 2006	25
Mar. 2004	22	July 2005	20	Nov. 2006	31
Apr. 2004	18	Aug. 2005	11	Dec. 2007	27
May 2004	Canceled	Sept. 2005	12	Mar. 2007	20
June 2004	15	Oct. 2005	29	Mar. 2007	10
July 2004	14	Nov. 2005	Canceled	Apr. 2007	18
Aug. 2004	12	Jan. 2006	20	Sept. 2007	13
Sept. 2004	4	Feb. 2006	20	Mar. 2008	12
Oct. 2004	5	Mar. 2006	17	July 2008	21
Nov. 2004	14	Apr. 2006	20	July 2009	10
Dec. 2004	8	May 2006	6	2010	-

Source: London Brights.
No meetings were held in 2010, according to the London Brights Web site.

54

The meetings were originally held monthly and attracted a slightly fluctuating attendance, which firmed up during 2006 and the first few months of 2007. This period overlapped roughly with the publication of the two most high-profile works of the New Atheism: Dawkins's *The God Delusion* (2006) and Hitchens's *God is Not Great* (2007). (Neither Harris nor Dennett really attracted much attention in the UK.) The site helpfully provides full details of each meeting, including estimates of attendance, occasionally with photographs allowing the number of attendees to be confirmed.

The December 2006 "Yuletide Celebration" social event was clearly much appreciated, whereas only four people responded to the following invitation in May 2006 to watch *The Da Vinci Code* together: "You know you want to see the film. So why not see it with a bunch of friendly Brights and atheists?"[38] Who would want to miss out on that?

From the second half of 2007, the meetups became increasingly infrequent. Whereas ten meetings were scheduled for 2005, there were only two meetups arranged for 2008 and only one for 2009. Nothing at all happened in 2010. As of January 2011, the next meetup had yet to be announced. This may have been due to organizational difficulties. Then again, it might point to a more fundamental loss of interest and commitment, reflecting the waning of the novelty value of "Bright" ideas.

Yet the feature of Table 1 most likely to attract readers'

attention is the number of people attending the meetups. Wolf's 2006 comment about the London events being the "largest" might suggest Bright audiences in the hundreds, possibly even the thousands, rivaling those of some of the capital city's liveliest churches. Yet the maximum attendance in that year—which also turned out to be the biggest in the meetup's history—was at a speaker meeting, cohosted by London Atheists and filmed by Channel 4, to discuss "Brights in the United Kingdom." How many attended? Thirty-three—even with the possibility of appearing on national television![39]

If this group of Brights is one of the largest, what does that say about the rest of them? Any church that garnered such meager attendances on such an infrequent basis would have been closed down years ago. Perhaps the future isn't quite as Bright as Dawkins had imagined. Or possibly these figures simply remind us that the real strength of the New Atheism lies in its Web-based communities. New Atheists tend to be members of online associations of solitary, anonymous Web surfers rather than of physical societies shaped by face-to-face encounters and relationships, where all are known by their real names.

But the fact remains that the term *Bright* just has not caught on, and it's not very difficult to figure out why. When launching the movement in the *New York Times* back in 2003, Daniel Dennett insisted that telling people that he was "a Bright" was "not a boast but a proud avowal of an inquisitive world view." Well, that's not how anyone else saw it. The opposite of *bright* is *dim*, a mildly offensive word that translates as "stupid." By choosing to use the label "Bright," atheists were widely seen to be claiming to be smarter than everyone else, reinforcing the emerging perception that this form of atheism was elitist and self-important.

As John Allen Paulos, an academic who comments for the ABC Network, remarked, "I don't think a degree in public relations is needed to expect that many people will construe the term as smug, ridiculous, and arrogant."[40] Even one of the leading New Atheists was repulsed: Christopher Hitchens openly criticized Dawkins and Dennett for their "cringe-making proposal that atheists should conceitedly nominate themselves to be called 'Brights.'"[41] I'm with Hitchens on this one. You're bright because of the quality of your reasoning, not its outcomes.

The choice of the term has thus turned out to be something of a public-relations disaster. How could so many of the New Atheism's leading representatives fail to see that the label would backfire so spectacularly? Or that the use of it would create the kind of mind-set that Dawkins and Dennett had declared to be one of the cardinal sins of religion?

Let me explain. In *The God Delusion*, Dawkins strongly expresses the view that the teachings of Jesus of Nazareth encourage the formation of "in-groups" and "out-groups."[42] The evidence for this is not robust. Christian readers of this section of his book found the absence of any reference to the parable of the good Samaritan—directed specifically *against* hostility toward out-groups—somewhat puzzling. At any rate, Dawkins is clear on what the problem is, even if his attempt to implicate Jesus in its genesis is decidedly flaky: "Religion is a label of in-group/out-group enmity and vendetta, not necessarily worse than other labels such as skin colour, language, or preferred football team, but often available when other labels are not."[43]

But what about the Brights? Dawkins and Dennett paint the Brights as the in-group and religionists as the out-group. How does that avoid social division and antagonism? It is just another "label of in-group/out-group enmity"—a continuation of, rather than a solution to, the problem.

We've looked briefly at some of the leading features of the New Atheism, most notably its defining hostility toward religion. But what of the ideas that underlie this hostility? In the chapters that follow, we'll consider three major themes that have become definitive of the movement: its critique of religious violence (chapter 3) and its appeals to reason (chapter 4) and to science (chapter 5) as the foundations of rational beliefs. We begin by addressing the question of religion and violence.

PART TWO

ENGAGING THE NEW ATHEISM: THREE CORE THEMES

3

VIOLENCE: WHEN
RELIGION GOES WRONG

In 1932, William Temple (1881–1944), archbishop of York and later of Canterbury, delivered a series of lectures at the University of Glasgow on the theme of religion. His tone was uncompromising. A strong case could be made, he declared, for suggesting that religion had done more harm than good to humanity; that "bad religion" was not only the most serious problem facing humanity in the modern world, but its chief enemy: "religion itself, when developed to real maturity, knows quite well that the first object of its condemnation is bad Religion, which is a totally different thing from irreligion, and can be a very much worse thing."[1]

Undoubtedly religion can go wrong, and when it does, it must be challenged and changed. The prophets of Israel and Jesus of Nazareth were, William Temple believed, reformers who called into question the religious conventions of their day. In a similar way, we could regard the New Atheist critique of religion as helpfully indicating where reformation might be needed in our own time. But where most people see religion as something that *can* go wrong, the New Atheism seems to see it as something that *is* wrong. End of discussion; the only solution is to get rid of it.

DOES RELIGION POISON EVERYTHING?

The idea that "religion poisons everything" has become deeply embedded within the New Atheism. Religion is the root of all evil—intrinsically and necessarily dangerous. Sam Harris offers his own decidedly maverick and selective readings of central religious texts—such as the Bible and the Qur'an—to demonstrate that they possess an innate propensity to generate violence. Yet while this sound bite resonated deeply with the fears of some secular opinion-makers in Western culture immediately following the 9/11 suicide attacks by Islamic fanatics, it fails to engage fully and comprehensively with facts. Everyone agrees that some forms of religion are bad, mad, and dangerous. But being discriminatory *about* religion suggests a level of maturity that being discriminatory *against* religion does not.

Perhaps for this reason, many New Atheists, when pressed

firmly in open debate and confronted with the findings of the scholarly research literature, will grudgingly concede that there's nothing intrinsically evil about belief in God. The problem, they believe, is that it can lead to fanaticism.

Clearly this is a legitimate concern, and we'll explore it in detail a little later on. But first we need to return to the New Atheists' failure to offer a firm definition of the term *religion*. Their lack of success turns out to be understandable, as we shall see.

"Religion": A False Universal

The first point to make is simple: *religion* is a false universal. Individual religions exist; religion as a universal category does not, however convenient it may be as a form of political or social shorthand. How did this misunderstanding come about? During the period of colonial expansion (roughly from the seventeenth century to the nineteenth), many Europeans came across world-views that differed from their own and chose to label them as religions. In fact, lots of these were better regarded as philosophies of life, such as Confucianism, and some were explicitly nontheistic or atheistic. But because of the eighteenth-century Enlightenment belief in a universal notion called religion, all ended up being forced into the same mold.

It's increasingly agreed that definitions of religion tend to reflect the agendas and biases of those who propose them (there is in fact still no definition of *religion* that commands scholarly assent).[2] Pluralism, in its more naive forms, holds that all religions represent equally valid responses to the same divine reality. The New Atheism, in its more naive forms, holds that all religions represent equally invalid and delusional responses to a fictional nonreality (or as Christopher Hitchens puts it, "all religions are versions of the same untruth"[3]). But in reality, the porous and imprecise concept of religion extends far beyond those who believe in God, embracing a wide range of beliefs and values.

RELIGION AND SPIRITUALITY

Since some religious traditions, such as Buddhism, have no notion of God, it's perfectly possible to propose that "religiosity" is rather different from "belief in God." This critical distinction blunts the force of the atheist critique of religion considerably. It also explains why Sam Harris, who bristles with hostility toward religions that believe in God—such as Christianity, Judaism, and Islam—goes soft on Eastern religions (and their Westernized variants). Harris's position here, that religion is bad and spirituality is good, has generated considerable concern within the New Atheist community, some dropping dark and ominous hints of his "unsoundness." Is Harris a true believer, or has he gone native and become a soft rationalist?

In a 2006 article in *New Humanist*, the Indian scholar Meera Nanda—a Hindu before her deconversion—argued that Harris illustrated a disturbing trend in the New Atheism: a tendency toward credulity. Some atheists, she suggested, start believing in anything after they give up believing in God. Nanda notes that Harris "trots out the widely shared view that Abrahamic faiths encourage violence against man and nature, while eastern spirituality promotes peace and harmony with fellow creatures."[4] Might this, she wondered, reflect his own spiritual beliefs, which he exempted from his critique of other religious traditions?

For Nanda, Harris is a covert religious believer, hiding behind a smokescreen of rationalism and science. "The mystical beliefs which Harris so approves of are every bit as unscientific, untestable and unverifiable as the religious belief he so aggressively attacks." Harris's criticism of theistic religions is simply clearing the ground for reaffirming "his own Dzogchen Buddhist and Advaita Vedantic Hindu spirituality."

Spirituality is the answer to Islam's and Christianity's superstitions and wars, he tells us. Spiritualism is not just good for your soul, it is good for your mind as well: it can make you "happy, peaceful and even wise."[5]

The distinction between religion and spirituality is actually rather more complicated than Harris suggests, some scholars arguing that spirituality is basically an individual-centered, privatized religion.[6] If that's so, what exactly is the problem with religion? Surely it's no longer that it is unscientific, untestable, and unverifiable, but rather that religion is an *institutional* or *social* phenomenon whereas spirituality is an *individual* one. This scholarly analysis is ill suited to Harris's sloganeering style of argument, but it is of fundamental importance to any serious attempt to understand the issues.

RELIGIONS AND WORLDVIEWS

A further distinction of importance, which the New Atheism singularly fails to make, needs to be drawn between a religion and a worldview. Both religions (such as Christianity) and secular worldviews (such as Marxism) demand allegiance from their followers. The most successful worldviews actually incorporate religious elements, even if they are fundamentally secular in their outlook—as in the former Soviet Union's use of quasi-religious rituals to mark essentially secular events.[7]

The historian Martin Marty, rightly noting the lack of any viable definition of *religion*, identifies five features that he holds to be characteristic: religion focuses our "ultimate concern," it builds community, it appeals to myth and symbol, it's enforced through rites and ceremonies, and it demands certain behaviors from its adherents. All five features, he records, are also characteristic of political movements.[8] It's not unreasonable to say that, if religion is dangerous on this basis, then so is politics. As has often been pointed out (most recently by the Italian historian Emilio Gentile), politics easily morphs into religion when it sees itself as being of ultimate importance.[9] There can be (and are) political fanatics, just as there can be (and are) religious fanatics. The problem is fanaticism, not religion itself. Indeed, the dark and aggressive tone of the New Atheist critique of religion suggests that fanaticism is not limited to those who defend religion.

The New Atheism, of course, argues that religious worldviews offer motivations for violence that are not paralleled elsewhere: for Harris and Hitchens, it's obvious that religious beliefs lead directly to suicide bombings. But where is their evidence for this? Why don't they engage with the many empirical studies of why people are driven to such action in the first place?[10] Are they perhaps aware that the scholarly literature does not lead to their preferred conclusions? Dawkins is rightly cautious at this point in *The God Delusion*, suggesting that religion may only be one of the factors involved.

As Robert Pape, professor of political science at the University of Chicago, demonstrated in his definitive 2005 account of the motivations of such attacks, based on surveys of every known case of suicide bombing since 1980, religious belief of any kind does not appear to be either a necessary nor a sufficient condition to create suicide bombers. There's "little connection between suicide terrorism and Islamic fundamentalism, or any one of the world's religions."[11] Pape's analysis of the evidence suggests rather that the fundamental motivation for suicide bombings appears to be political—namely, the desire to force the withdrawal of foreign forces occupying land believed to belong to an oppressed people, who have seriously limited military resources at their disposal. His was an important study, which cast doubt on some of the fundamental assumptions of American foreign policy, particularly in the Middle East and the Caucasus. It also has obvious implications for wider debates about the relation of religion and terror.

Another important study approaches this question from an anthropological perspective. Scott Atran of the University of Michigan suggests that the way to stop suicide bombings is not by ridiculing or suppressing religion but by empowering religious moderates.[12]

As religious-studies scholar Richard E. Wentz points out in *Why People Do Bad Things in the Name of Religion*, the real issue here is absolutism[13] (the ethical view that certain actions are absolutely right or wrong)—an opinion echoed by the sociologist Alberto Toscano in his recent analysis of the history of fanaticism.[14] Toscano writes that religion is not the only thing to have created fanatics: politics and ideologies have, too, and continue to do so. He shows how the tension between fanaticism and reasonableness is constructed by power groups, with vested interests in mind. His analysis of the "fanaticism" of the eighteenth-century Enlightenment will make uncomfortable reading for those—such as Harris and Hitchens—who naively believe that the best hope for the human race is a return to the Enlightenment.

CHRISTIANITY AND NONVIOLENCE

Any discussion about religious violence must take into account the inconvenient fact that Christianity offers a transcendent rationale for the *resistance* of violence. Christians hold that the nature of God is made known in Jesus of Nazareth,[15] so the words and actions of Jesus reveal the character and will of God. For this reason, it's important to note that Jesus demonstrated a commitment to nonviolence in both his teachings and actions.[16] He was the object, not the agent, of violence. Similarly, instead of meeting violence with violence, rage with rage, Christians are asked to turn the other cheek and not to let the sun go down on their anger (Matthew 5:39; Ephesians 4:26). Now, I have no doubt that lots of

Christians fail to behave like this. But maybe that just shows that they are not very good Christians.

Christianity will always stand in constant need of reformation. Christian churches have used or condoned violence in the past and are rightly to be criticized for doing so. Christian institutions need repeatedly to call themselves back to reflect on the core ideas and values of Jesus. One inspiring example of a lived-out ethos of nonviolence, grounded in the Christian faith, is that which undergirded Martin Luther King Jr.'s campaign for civil rights.

Another may be seen in the Amish schoolhouse killings of October 2006. A gunman broke into an Amish school in the village of Nickel Mines in the state of Pennsylvania and gunned down a group of schoolgirls. Five of the young girls died. The gunman shot himself at the scene, leaving a suicide note that declared that he was "filled with so much hate" against God.

The Amish are a conservative Protestant religious group who repudiate any form of violence on account of their understanding of the absolute moral authority of the person and teaching of Jesus of Nazareth. Despite the brutal force used against the most vulnerable members of their community by a man with a grudge against God, the Amish community urged forgiveness. There would be no violence, no revenge—only the offering of forgiveness.[17] The gunman's widow spoke, gratefully and movingly, of how this provided the "healing" that she and her three children "so desperately needed." The cycle of violence was thus broken before it began.

This tragic story, marked by nobility and dignity, is unquestionably a challenge to the churches to bring their ethics into line with those of their founder. But it's an even greater challenge to the plausibility of the New Atheist critique of religion as intrinsically violent. Jesus of Nazareth just doesn't fit that mold, and neither should Christianity.

Atheist Violence Against Religion

It's time to explore another theme, which is conveniently glossed over by the New Atheist manifestos: what about atheist violence against religion? As someone who grew up in Northern Ireland, I know only too well how religion can generate violence. But religion is not alone in this. Any worldview based on an exclusivist metanarrative (a controlling story) has the potential to provoke hostility.

The history of the twentieth century has made us frighteningly aware of how political extremism can cause violence and makes grim reading (unless you airbrush out the bits you don't like or won't accept). Never before in human history had so many people been massacred in the name of so many secular ideologies, metanarratives, and visions of progress. Yet all of these reflected a post-religious secular ideology—whether it was the quasi-paganism of Nazism or the atheism of Stalinism. If the eighteenth-century Enlightenment is to be seen as the liberation of Western societies from the tyranny of religion and theocratic rule (a standard element of the New Atheist apologetic), the twentieth century has made clear that the violence and cruelty of God-fearing societies are more than adequately matched by that of their godless alternatives.

That's one of the reasons that postmodernity is so critical of such metanarratives in the first place. Though the rejection of these controlling stories is itself deeply problematic, seeming to give rise to incoherence, writers such as Jean-François Lyotard argue that their propensity to generate oppression, exclusion, and violence is so great that they are to be resisted as a matter of principle. I do concede that Christianity can generate violence; so, too, can Marxism and the New Atheism, the latter precisely because its metanarrative has been constructed to account for— and hence to argue for the elimination of—religious alternatives.

An antireligious metanarrative was deeply embedded in the ideology of the Soviet Union, the world's first officially atheistic state.[18] Its founder, V. I. Lenin, always regarded the intellectual, cultural, and physical elimination of religion as central to the socialist revolution and had identified atheism as an essential element of his ideology long before the Bolshevik Revolution of October 1917. In laying down how the revolutionary cause was to be advanced within Russia, he wrote, "Our propaganda necessarily includes the propaganda of atheism."[19] In an attempt to win over the people through argument, Lenin suggested that it was necessary "to translate and widely disseminate the literature of the eighteenth-century French Enlighteners and atheists."

Yet Lenin was reluctant to draw attention to the fact that an institutionalized atheism lay at the heart of his revolutionary program, fearing its implications for the popular acceptance of his aims. "We do not and should not set forth our atheism in our Program," he noted. Why not? Because he hoped to win religious people over through political means.

The Bolshevik Revolution gave Lenin the opportunity to implement his political and religious objectives. When religious belief conspicuously and obstinately failed to disappear as a result of social and political change, he eventually put in place measures designed to eradicate it through the "protracted use of violence." One of the greatest tragedies of this dark era in human history was that those who sought to eliminate faith through violence and oppression believed that they were justified in doing so.[20] They were accountable to no higher authority than the state.

A key player in this atheist crusade was the League of

Militant Atheists, a semiofficial coalition of various political forces that operated within the Soviet Union from 1925 to 1947.[21] With the slogan "The Struggle Against Religion Is a Struggle for Socialism," the group set out to destroy the credibility of religion through social, cultural, and intellectual manipulation. Its carefully orchestrated campaigns involved using newspapers, journals, lectures, and films to persuade Soviet citizens that religious beliefs and practices were irrational and destructive. Good Soviet citizens, they declared, ought to embrace a scientific, atheistic worldview.

Churches were closed or destroyed, often by dynamiting; priests were imprisoned, exiled, or executed. On the eve of the Second World War, there were only 6,376 clergy remaining in the Russian Orthodox Church, compared with the prerevolutionary figure of 66,140. One dreadful day, February 17, 1938, saw the execution of fifty-five priests. In 1917, there were 39,530 churches in Russia; by 1940, only 950 remained functional.

The New Atheist response to this grim history is widely seen as unsatisfactory. It goes like this: maybe Stalin was a vicious atheist thug, but he was a vicious thug who just happened to be an atheist. Furthermore, what made him a vicious thug was his seminary training. Anyway, these atheist states weren't really atheist at all! Christopher Hitchens argues that the Soviet Union was really a *religious* state, which explains why it was so immoral and violent. Communism became a religion—and that's when things turned nasty.[22]

The tenuous thought processes underlying Hitchens's confident declarations here are rather difficult to discern, but they seem to run like this:

Major premise: religion is evil and violent.
Minor premise: the Soviet Union was evil and violent.
Conclusion: the Soviet Union was therefore religious.

We move from fiction ("all religion is evil") to pure fantasy ("all evil is religious"), everything being forced into the ideological mold by Hitchens's dogged belief in the intrinsic violence and evil of religion.[23] He does not engage with the substantial body of literature now available concerning the suppression of religion during the Soviet Union (especially from 1925 to 1947), or show any awareness of its implications for his somewhat problematic reading of history.

Yet Hitchens does not stand alone as an uncritical New Atheist observer of state atheism, such as that of the Soviet Union. Richard Dawkins insists that there's "not the smallest evidence" that atheism systematically influences people to do bad things,[24] and that he does "not believe there is an atheist in the world who would bulldoze Mecca—or Chartres, York Minster or Notre Dame."[25] Unfortunately, this noble sentiment reflects his personal credulity rather than the reality of things. What he believes is irrelevant; the facts speak for themselves. From 1925 onward, the League of Militant Atheists urged the burning and dynamiting of huge numbers of churches, including some of great cultural importance. All were doomed to be swept out of the way as reminders of an earlier age of faith. Moscow would be a "multi-story city of iron" looking to the future, not the past.[26]

Similar outrages can be found in the postwar history of the German Democratic Republic (better known as "East Germany"). The University Church of St. Paul in Leipzig, an architectural masterpiece completed in 1240, was blown up in May 1968 to avoid the awkwardness of having to tolerate symbols of the divine in the new "Karl Marx Platz."[27] (This is now renamed the "Augustinerplatz," following the collapse of this grim and miserable Marxist state in 1990, which embodied precisely the austere dogmatic atheism that some New Atheists seem to regard as an intellectual virtue.) Happily, the church was reconstructed in 2009 in response to public demand.

Dawkins gives every impression of being in denial about the darker side of atheism, making him a less than credible critic of religion. Just where in this analysis do we find the rigorous evidence-based thinking he commends and commands? Dawkins has a fervent, pious, and unquestioning faith in the universal goodness of atheism that he refuses to subject to critical examination.

SECULAR IDEALS AND VIOLENCE

An important point made by some New Atheists is that religion—or, if we're to avoid exaggeration, certain *forms* of religion—can possess a capacity to transcendentalize normal human conflicts and disagreements, thus transforming them into cosmic battles of good and evil in which the authority and will of a transcendent reality is implicated. Religious conflicts are thus argued to have an intensity lacking in their secular counterparts.

Yet when a society rejects the idea of God, it tends to transcendentalize secular alternatives, such as the ideals of liberty or equality. As the Italian political theorist Emilio Gentile rightly points out, worldviews arise that, though secular in their outlooks, nevertheless take the form of "a more or less developed system of beliefs, myths, rituals, and symbols that create an aura of sacredness around an entity belonging to this world and turn it into a cult and an object of worship and devotion."[28] The result is inevitable—a tendency toward intolerance and violence when such secular "objects of worship and devotion" are challenged or threatened.

A good example of this development can be seen in the "Reign of Terror" of 1794 following the onset of the French Revolution (motto: "Liberty, Equality, Fraternity"), which arose directly out of the secular political ideologies of that age. This shocking episode saw doctrinaire disputes between the Jacobins and Girondins claim thousands of lives through mass executions of "enemies of the revolution" in one year.[29] Maximilien Robespierre, reasoning that terror was virtuous because it attempted to maintain the Revolution and the Republic, declared that "terror is nothing else than swift, severe, inexorable justice; it flows from virtue."[30] In other words, it's a *rational* as opposed to a *religious* form of violence. (I wonder if Sam Harris has been inspired by this historical example in his puzzling and troubling defense of rational violence.) Safeguarding the Revolution and Republic justified whatever means were necessary to this end. Robespierre himself eventually fell victim to the same rational terror he'd unleashed and defended. Having fallen out of favor, he was sent to the guillotine in 1794.

All ideals—divine, transcendent, human, or invented—are capable of being abused. They can easily become the end that justifies the means needed to achieve them—including the elimination of people and ideas that are held to be dangerous to their survival or success. New Atheists tend to be a little vague about this, but they certainly seem to encourage the idea that once we get rid of religion, we get rid of some nasty violence. There's just no evidence for this. Two points need to be made in response.

First, the vicious "wars of religion" of the seventeenth century were replaced by the equally vicious but infinitely more destructive ideological and nationalistic wars of the twentieth.

The erosion of religion as a social force in Western Europe did not lead to the peaceful coexistence imagined by the more idealistic rationalists of the Enlightenment. The First World War, as is often pointed out, had no religious dimension.

And second, human beings are very good at inventing ways of distinguishing themselves from other groups of human beings and allowing these differences to generate conflict. Religion is one such difference. But there are lots of others: gender, class, ethnicity, sexual orientation, language, and football. Get rid of religion, and conflict and violence will simply find other occasions for their emergence and other grounds for their justification.

Where do these reflections take us? I believe we must make a plea for realism and get away from the superficiality of recent public debates in which carefully nuanced and evidence-based scholarly analyses of the nature of religion—and its impact on society and human well-being—seem to have been swept to one side in a cultural war driven by headlines and sound bites.

Secular humanism appeals to the best of humanity in defining itself. So why should it not also examine the best in religion in defending itself? Of course religion can go wrong, but so can just about anything. For example, science has been grossly abused—witness the forms of "social Darwinism" that emerged in Nazi Germany, now widely condemned as an abomination yet seen as progressive by many social liberals at the time. I'm perfectly prepared to accept that this is bad science and not to judge science by its bastardizations. Both science and religion can spawn monsters, but they need not do so, nor should either be judged by its pathological forms.

The New Atheism has simply failed to make its case that religion is necessarily and uniformly evil, mad, or destructive. Harris, Dawkins, and Hitchens offer antireligious narratives of such embarrassing selectivity that they make even some New Atheists cringe with discomfort. As Terry Eagleton remarked of the pastiche of material assembled in Dawkins's *The God Delusion*, "Such is Dawkins's unruffled scientific impartiality that in a book of almost four hundred pages, he can scarcely bring himself to concede that a single human benefit has flowed from religious faith, a view which is as a priori improbable as it is empirically false."[31]

I'm all for religion being corrected and reformed, but I do think the New Atheism might show a similar willingness to subject itself to self-searching intellectual and moral criticisms and be a little more honest about its own problems.

4

REASON: THE RATIONALITY
OF BELIEFS

I n January 1697, the great English philosopher John Locke
wrote to his close friend William Molyneux, celebrating
the joy of the pursuit of truth in life: "I know there is truth
opposite to falsehood, that it may be found if people will, and
is worth the seeking, and is not only the most valuable, but the
pleasantest thing in the world."[1] I keep coming back to Locke's
words, which I find a constant source of inspiration. They could
serve as the motto for science, philosophy, and theology—and
indeed for the New Atheism, which I'm sure shares in this hon-
orable and noble quest for truth in a puzzling and ambiguous
world. Yet the New Atheism's critics, including many atheists,
argue that New Atheism seems to think it has a monopoly on
truth, refusing as a matter of principle to concede the rationality
of other positions, above all of religious faith.

I love reason and science. I'm a freethinker. That's what led me to give up on my earlier atheism and embrace the Christian faith while studying the natural sciences at university back in 1971. I have no doubt that Richard Dawkins is a freethinker too. Yet Dawkins and I seem to understand the notions of reason and science in rather different ways, and I find that our freethinking leads to very different conclusions.

But that's just the way things are. Reason, as Dante noted, has "short wings."[2] Philosophers are still debating the great questions of truth and have yet to settle their differences. Is there a reality outside our minds? Is there a God? What is the good life? The jury is out on all these and countless other issues. But that doesn't stop us making decisions about what we believe to be the best answers and basing our lives on them. Maybe that's one good reason that we should be respectful of differences and refrain from dismissing those who disagree with us.

The 2003 discussion between two leading academics—atheist Jack Smart and theist John Haldane—was a superb illustration of a principled, courteous, and informed debate on the issues. Both scholars conceded the rationality of the other's position while arguing for the superiority of their own.[3] There was no question of Smart lapsing into the kind of dismissive and superficial assertions Sam Harris has been known to make, or of Haldane defending the "irrationality" of faith in ways that Dawkins or Dennett seem to think is characteristic of religious belief. Both positions were seen as worthy of support by thinking and intelligent people. The debate is—as it's always been—still wide open.

In the next two chapters we'll look critically at reason and science—both vital tools in our engagement with reality—and explore how they relate to the New Atheism. It's important to remember that every tool needs to be calibrated before use. How reliable is it? Are there conditions under which it malfunctions, producing false positives or distorted results? What are its operating limits? Good tools, when badly used, lead to unreliable outcomes. The wise person knows the limits of the methods being employed to get results. Otherwise, the results cannot be trusted.

This important idea of being critical about reason is not new. Immanuel Kant and David Hume, two leading philosophers of the eighteenth-century Enlightenment, were quite clear that reason had its limits and that these had to be identified and respected.[4] Both were deeply skeptical about capacity of reason to solve metaphysical problems. Reason might be good at critiquing views it perceived to be irrational, but that didn't mean that it could construct alternative visions of reality of its own.

The New Atheism makes rationality one of its core defining characteristics and emphatically and aggressively denies that any alternative view can be regarded as rational. It needs to be said, however, that this is a populist rather than a scholarly view. Most reflective atheists outside the New Atheism concede both the limits of reason and the rationality of non-atheistic perspectives. They may believe that their atheism makes more sense than its alternatives, but they certainly won't necessarily dismiss belief in God as irrational.

THE RATIONALITY OF BELIEF IN GOD

The twentieth century has seen philosophers of religion, such as Alvin Plantinga and Richard Swinburne, reaffirm the rationality of faith and reinvigorate traditional debates about reasons for belief in God—catalyzed in part by new scientific understandings of the origins of the universe. There's a growing consensus that belief in God is perfectly rational—unless, of course, you define *rationality* in terms that deliberately exclude such a belief.[5]

Rationality is less concerned with adopting a particular starting point or conclusion than with the rules that regulate reflective discussion leading to a conclusion. New Atheist writers often define the term beyond its fundamental sense, holding that it demands we interpret the world in a specific way that excludes belief in God. Yet this interpretation clearly involves smuggling in a host of value judgments, assumptions, and unverifiable starting points about the nature of reality that are, strictly speaking, not demonstrable by reason. Here, for example, in a rather colorful passage from a lecture given at the Edinburgh Festival some years ago, Richard Dawkins asserts that religious faith is simply and necessarily a revolt against reason and evidence:

> Faith is the great cop-out, the great excuse to evade the need to think and evaluate evidence. Faith is belief in spite of, even perhaps because of, the lack of evidence. . . . Faith is not allowed to justify itself by argument.[6]

Dawkins seems to overlook the legion of religious writers—such as Richard Swinburne and C. S. Lewis—who insisted that faith could and should justify itself by argument. Perhaps some religious people do refuse to think. My studies of New Atheist Web sites lead me to believe they're not alone in that. But it's just nonsense to represent this as *typical* of either religion or atheism.

But where is there any recognition of the limits of reason? In debate with Dawkins, he once challenged me to prove—by science or reason—that there is a God. If I could prove it, he would believe it. Unfortunately it's not that simple! As will become clear in this chapter and the next, there are in fact rather *few* things that can be proved by reason or science, and God isn't one of them. Nor, for that matter, is anything else of ultimate importance—including the core values and ideas of atheism.

The great British philosopher and intellectual historian Sir Isaiah Berlin (1909–97) pointed out some years ago that human convictions can be grouped together under three categories:

1. Those that can be established by empirical observation
2. Those that can be established by logical deduction
3. Those that cannot be proved in either of these ways[7]

The first two categories concern what can be known reliably through the natural sciences on the one hand, and what can be proved through logic and mathematics on the other. The third category concerns the values and ideas that have shaped human culture and given human existence direction and purpose, but cannot be proved by reason or science.[8]

What sort of values and ideas? Here's one. In 1948, the United Nations "reaffirmed their faith in fundamental human rights." The statements of the Universal Declaration of Human Rights, such as "All human beings are born free and equal in dignity and rights. They are endowed with reason and conscience and should act towards one another in a spirit of brotherhood" cannot be proved, logically or scientifically; nor can the belief that democracy is better than fascism, or that oppression is evil. But many noble and wise people make upholding such things their life's work, trusting that they are, in the first place, right, and in the second, important. Nobody thinks they're mad for doing so. As the literary critic Terry Eagleton rightly points out, "We hold many beliefs that have no unimpeachably rational justification, but are nonetheless reasonable to entertain."[9]

The philosopher Alvin Plantinga made this point years ago with reference to the perennial philosophical problem of "other minds."[10] To explain briefly: while I have direct knowledge that I have a mind, I can't absolutely prove that you, the reader, have a mind, and you can't absolutely prove that other people have minds. But nobody's unduly bothered about this. It's a safe assumption for us to make, and it chimes in with the way things seem to be. Plantinga argues for a parallel between proving the existence of "other minds" and proving the existence of God. Neither can be verified, and good arguments can be raised against both—but to their defenders, both seem entirely reasonable.

The New Atheism refuses to confront the inconvenient truth that every worldview—whether religious or secular—goes beyond what reason or science can prove. That's just the way things are. The "ultimate questions" about value and meaning won't go away. Both the New Atheism and Christianity represent and rest upon convictions. Both are based on what they know cannot be proved yet nevertheless hold to be trustworthy. As has often been pointed out, that's how worldviews and belief systems—whether religious or secular—work.

> All such ultimate questions and their answers about life and death, sin and suffering, hope and healing, finally elude our intellectual grasp and strict logical proof. In the end we say simply, "I am doing this because I believe that this is the nature of life and that my ultimate happiness depends on my acting in accord with my deepest commitment and dearest beliefs."[11]

Christopher Hitchens declares boldly that New Atheists such as himself do not entertain beliefs—"Our belief is not a belief."[12] It's one of the best examples of blind faith I've come across—a delusion that makes his whole approach vulnerable. To give one obvious example: Hitchens's anti-theism rests on certain moral values (such as "religion is evil" or "God is not good") that he is unable to demonstrate by reason. Hitchens simply assumes that his moral values are shared by his sympathetic readers, who are unlikely to ask inconvenient questions about their origins, foundations, or reliability. When he's called upon to prove them (as he regularly is in debates), he finds himself unable to do so. His beliefs are indeed beliefs, even if he prefers not to concede this decisive point. Welcome to the human race, Mr. Hitchens. That's the position we're all in—including you.

HUMAN REASON AND THE INVENTION OF GOD

For Christian writers, religious faith is not a rebellion against reason but a revolt against the imprisonment of humanity within the cold walls of a rationalist dogmatism. Logic and facts can only "take us so far; then we have to go the rest of the way toward belief."[13] Human logic may be rationally adequate, but it's also existentially deficient. Faith declares that there's more to life than this. It doesn't contradict reason but transcends it. It elicits and invites rational consent but does not compel it. Unfortunately, some of those who boast of being freethinkers are simply imprisoned by a defunct eighteenth-century rationalism, unaware of the radical changes in our understanding of rationality that have emerged in the last fifty years.[14]

Many New Atheists will quite reasonably want to protest at this point. From a New Atheist perspective, it's not that human reason discovers God by reaching beyond reason but that naive human beings invent God. More than that: they invent a nasty God. Let's reflect on this important objection in more detail.

According to New Atheist Web sites, this invented God is to be blamed for the evil of the world. It's not the fault of decent human beings. God is a revolting oppressor, more to be compared to a North Korean dictator than to a good shepherd. This fundamental criticism is summed up clearly, if a little portentously, by Richard Dawkins:

The God of the Old Testament is arguably the most unpleasant character in all fiction: jealous and proud of it; a petty, unjust, unforgiving control-freak; a vindictive, bloodthirsty ethnic cleanser; a misogynistic, homophobic, racist, infanticidal, genocidal, filicidal, pestilential, megalomaniacal, sadomasochistic, capriciously malevolent bully.[15]

It may be a clumsy piece of prose, but there's no denying the rage it expresses, which Dawkins is careful to present as reflecting his moral outrage rather than antireligious prejudice. There's no point in understanding or tolerating religions when they submit to such a repulsive deity. The important thing is to resist them and purge such hideous ideas from society at large.

New Atheist bloggers frequently speculate on the moral turpitude and degeneracy of this invented deity. Some even go so far as to declare that God was the hidden force that locked the doors of the Auschwitz gas chambers and poured in the cyanide. But let's think about this for a moment. As a made-up concept, God could not possibly tell people to close the doors of the gas chambers and pour in the gas. Nor, for that matter, could God tell people to kill vast numbers of innocent people in an act of terrorism such as 9/11. Within its own intellectual framework, God is simply not an intellectual option for the New Atheism. God is a delusion. People are deluded in believing in God. If the New Atheism is right, there is no God to tell people to do *anything*.

Yet the doors of the gas chambers were still closed, and the gas was still poured in. And 9/11 happened. If there's no God, these things simply cannot be God's fault. They were acts committed by human beings. The New Atheism may protest that they were committed by *deluded* human beings. But there's no escaping the dreadful and inconvenient truth: if there's no God, then there's no one to dump the blame on for human evil. The fault is ours alone.

The New Atheism, in scapegoating God for the rational and moral failings of human beings, is hoping that nobody will notice the blatant incoherence in its own worldview. Everything that's wrong with the world, it assures us, can be blamed on God. But if God is an invention, a fictional character, then the blame has to be laid firmly and squarely at the door of God's human creators. It wasn't God who initiated or executed the Holocaust. It was human beings in the twentieth century, supposedly at the zenith of their rationality and morality. The New Atheism needs to get used to this and start making some adjustments.

Classical atheist critiques of religion argue that gods look just like their creators.[16] Human beings create God in their own likeness, attributing their own moral and rational qualities to these allegedly supernatural beings.[17] Hitchens himself endorses this view and provides a snappy little summary of it: "God did not create man in his own image. Evidently, it was the other way about."[18] Or alternatively: "the mildest criticism of religion is also the most radical and the most devastating one. Religion is man-made."[19] Yet if the New Atheism is right about the moral delinquency of God or religion, Hitchens's conclusion doesn't exactly portray humanity in a very good light. Maybe it's not that religion corrupts humanity but that a corrupt humanity creates a look-alike religion.

So let's rewrite Dawkins's piece about the God of the Old Testament, retaining its style while making the crucial point above, which raises very difficult questions for the New Atheist way of looking at things:

The God of the Old Testament is arguably the most unpleasant character in all fiction, created by equally unpleasant human beings who were jealous and proud of it; who were petty, unjust, unforgiving control freaks; who were vindictive, bloodthirsty ethnic cleansers; who were misogynistic, homophobic, racist, infanticidal, genocidal, filicidal, pestilential, megalomaniacal, sadomasochistic, capriciously malevolent bullies; and who created their gods in their own image.

The New Atheism is in an intellectually and morally uncomfortable place. The more it excoriates religion as irrational and immoral, the more it highlights the irrationality and immorality of its creators. It's caught in a dilemma framed and created by two of its core beliefs (neither of which, of course, can be proved):

1. God is evil and nasty.
2. God is a delusion created by human beings.

As I read Hitchens and Dawkins, I sometimes find myself wondering if they would actually prefer God to exist. Their ferocious anger and their litany of complaints would then be directed against a real being who could be hauled before his accusers and held to account. If the ferocity of some

New Atheist writers and bloggers is anything to go by, God would probably get lynched. (Come to think of it, wasn't that what happened when the mob turned against Jesus Christ and demanded his crucifixion?) God can be scapegoated for everything that's wrong with society, and that allows some people to feel better about themselves. But if there's no God, the spotlight of blame shifts relentlessly onto us.

The real problem for secular rationalists is that having made human beings the "measure of all things,"[20] they find themselves embarrassed by the range of convictions human beings have chosen to hold—most notably, the widespread belief in God. If belief in God is a human invention, and if the crimes committed in the name of religion are thus of human origin, humanity appears to be rather less rational and moral than the New Atheist worldview allows.

The "Bright" and the Redemption of Rationality

But there's a way of getting around this problem for the New Atheism. To explain this, we need to return to the idea of the "Bright," which we introduced in chapter 2. This elitist notion became something of a public relations embarrassment for the New Atheism, solidifying the growing view that the movement was intellectually conceived. Nevertheless, the idea of the Bright is completely consistent with the New Atheist metanarrative, which often takes a strongly dualist turn, especially on atheist blogs. Humanity is here divided into two camps: those who rely on reason and science and those lesser mortals who are credulous and superstitious. According to this controlling set of ideas, people who still believe in God are intellectually and morally deficient. They're the irrational and immoral villains who caused religion to come into existence in the first place and continue to support it today.

Although Hitchens refuses to use the term *Bright*, a similar idea is central to his analysis. The biblical authors were, as Hitchens rather disdainfully puts it, "crude, uncultured human mammals."[21] Yet this radical division of humanity reinforces the growing perception that the New Atheism—which must here be distinguished from the gracious, moderate, tolerant, and informed atheism of writers such as Alain Badiou, Julian Baggini, John Gray, and Slavoj Žižek—looks and sounds awfully like a form of religious fundamentalism.

The fundamentalist mind-set, whether religious or secular, is characterized by a dogmatic certainty about its beliefs that fails to acknowledge the limitations under which human reasoning operates. Fundamentalisms divide the world into two rigid categories—the saved and the damned (if you're religious) or the rationalist and superstitious (if you're secular). There's no spectrum of alternative or intermediary possibilities, no *tertium quid*.

But if the New Atheism is angered by "moderate atheists" who don't fit into its maps of meaning, it's happy enough to align itself with moderate atheists when it suits its purposes, using the high repute of writers such as Iris Murdoch to deflect charges of intellectual vapidity or argumentative deficiency. Unfortunately, I see nothing of Murdoch's personal graciousness, philosophical skills, or wisdom about the human situation reflected in the New Atheism. Her emphasis upon the human capacity to deceive itself,[22] accepting illusions as if they were reality, has much to say to Dawkins, Hitchens, and their colleagues. They assert that religious people are deluded in their beliefs about God, but what about their own beliefs about human nature? Or the foundations of ethics? As Murdoch once quipped, "One should go easy on smashing other people's lies. Better to concentrate on one's own."[23]

An alternative New Atheist strategy is to argue that humanity has grown up since the age in which religion began to flourish. It wasn't that humanity was *originally* irrational in believing in God; that just seemed the best way of making sense of things back in the Bronze Age when nobody knew any better. But what of the situation now? Numerically, far more people believe in God today than ever did in the past.

The New Atheist dilemma concerns why so many human beings *continue* to hold to such belief when they have no business doing so.

Once more, the concept of the Bright comes to the rescue. Those who break free from the past and assert the gospel of atheism are the illuminated elite, while the persistence of religion can be put down to unenlightened individuals rebelling against the dictates of reason and science, perniciously defending the indefensible when they know it to be wrong—or being so dim and unperceptive that they fail to understand what reason and science are saying in the first place.

To critics of the New Atheism, this comes across as nauseatingly arrogant; within movement itself, as I've discovered from numerous conversations, it's seen as self-evidently true. Outsiders are fools or knaves; true enlightenment is only found within its hallowed Bright walls. Believing that the rest of humanity is deluded does, I fear, generate a certain unpleasant smugness on the part of these "true believers."

THE ENLIGHTENMENT AND THE NEW ATHEISM

The ideals of the Enlightenment play an important part in the thinking of New Atheist writers. Indeed, critics of the New Atheism have not been slow to point out that it's incorrigibly wedded to modernism, a cultural mood that's now in retreat.[24] In line with this modernist commitment, Richard Dawkins is highly critical of postmodernism, regarding it as irrational twaddle and believing that a return to the Enlightenment would put an end to all this nonsense. Christopher Hitchens portrays the Enlightenment in an embarrassingly triumphalist manner—as a bold and brilliant period in Western culture in which reason and science overthrew the tyranny of religion, tradition, prejudice, and superstition. Humanity, we're told, began to think for itself and threw out the junk in its attic—such as God.

But while the New Atheism tends to present the Enlightenment as a reaction against God, it could arguably be more accurately regarded as a quest to liberate human institutions and ideas from external authority (such as the state or church), and ground them on a universal rational foundation, which would command assent by force of evidence, not by force of arms.[25] The identification of such a secure and universal basis of knowledge would free society from incessant disagreements and recurrent violence, such as that experienced during the Thirty Years' War (1618–48).

The Enlightenment asked all the right questions and challenged a series of traditional attitudes and beliefs that were in radical need of overhaul. For a while it looked as if it might actually work. Human reason could sort out all the great questions of life without the need to appeal to a higher authority—or, indeed, to any other authority. But by the outbreak of the First World War, it was obvious that the Enlightenment quest for truth was in deep trouble. Why?

One major concern was that the Enlightenment's appeal to reason as the ultimate reliable source of authority could not be verified. How could it possibly be checked out to make sure it was reliable? Some retorted that reason itself could demonstrate its own authority. But to its critics, this was unpersuasive. Surely such a defense of the authority of human reason was ultimately circular and parasitical, assuming and depending upon its own conclusions. If there was a flaw in human reasoning processes, reason itself would not be able to detect this. We'd be locked into unreliable patterns of thought without any means of escape. Some say rationalism liberates. Wiser souls suggest that it has the capacity to entrap and imprison.

The recent rise of postmodernity is really not a symptom of irrationalism (as Hitchens and Dawkins assert) but a protest against the existential inadequacy of rationalism and the authoritarianism it has encouraged. People came to realize the manifest deficiencies of an approach to life that's determined—as opposed to being merely informed— by reason, and they protested against those who tried to shoehorn them into a rationalist cage.

The work of the Austrian mathematician and philosopher

Kurt Gödel (1906–78) gave a new rigor to these concerns. While he was only twenty-five years old, Gödel set out his "incompleteness theorem." Although Gödel's theorems were primarily mathematical, it was obvious they had profound philosophical implications, not least in demonstrating the inability of reason to prove its own competency. One of Gödel's more recent interpreters here explains the importance of his work:

> How can a person, operating within a system of beliefs, including beliefs about beliefs, get outside that system to determine whether it is rational? If your entire system becomes infected with madness, including the very rules by which you reason, then how can you ever reason your way out of madness?[26]

Gödel's analysis reinforced the growing realization that reason *cannot* be used to establish its own authority and competence. This point is simply evaded by those who speak loosely and naively of freethinking, unaware of the capacity of reason to delude, limit, and imprison. Reason is constrained.

Other concerns can easily be added to this. More recent philosophical critics of the Enlightenment—such as Alasdair MacIntyre or John Gray—have argued that its quest for a universal foundation and criterion of knowledge faltered, stumbled, and finally crumbled as it became clear it just couldn't deliver what it promised.[27] For MacIntyre, this meant that human beings need to realize that they have to reason and live in the absence of any clear, unambiguous, absolute, and purely rational truths. We must indeed articulate and defend criteria by which our beliefs may be justified, but also realize that those beliefs may lie beyond proof. They are, to use a phrase popularized by the Harvard psychologist William James, to be regarded as "working hypotheses."[28]

These concerns about the reliability of human reason, and its capacity to resolve the great questions of life consistently and authoritatively, are given added urgency by the writings of Karl Marx, Charles Darwin, and Sigmund Freud. Let's explore why.

WHAT ABOUT MARX, DARWIN, AND FREUD?

In the last two centuries, Karl Marx (1818–83), Charles Darwin (1809–82), and Sigmund Freud (1856–1939) have raised questions that are deeply troubling to those wedded to exaggerated forms of rationalism that stress the autonomy and reliability of unaided human reason.

Let's look first at the issues raised by Karl Marx. One of his basic assertions is that human ideas are fundamentally shaped by cultural factors, above all social and economic conditions.

Ideas are the superstructure erected upon—and perhaps even ultimately determined by—a socioeconomic base.[29] The New Atheism points out that Marx and his followers declared God to be a social construction, reflecting human social alienation. Yet it conveniently chooses to ignore that Marx's approach is universal in scope, and that if he's right, *all* our ideas are covertly molded by our contexts—including atheism. We do not have control over them, as rationalist thinkers once believed. While the New Atheism would like us to think of Marx criticizing religion as the "opium of the people," his thought is just as corrosive to the Enlightenment rationalism undergirding New Atheist ideas.

It's no criticism of certain leading representatives of the eighteenth-century Enlightenment to suggest that they must now be seen as sociologically naive. Enlightenment thinkers couldn't be expected to understand how deeply human beliefs and practices are embedded in a social and cultural context, a perception that only began to emerge in the late nineteenth century.[30] But now that we're aware of it, there's no going back. The rise of the New Atheism, and the specific forms it took, are clearly conditioned by its historical context.

As if social and cultural conditioning were not enough, we also have to contend with the Freudian argument that we do not have access to our own true motivations. Our actions and ideas are shaped by dark forces within our subconsciousness that we do not really understand and find difficult to overcome. If reason is shaped by our sub-conscious yearnings and passions, might it not imprison rather than liberate us?

A real problem for those who believe that reason *can* liberate us relates to contemporary interpretations of evolutionary theory. Charles Darwin is often adopted as a popular mascot by the New Atheism. For example, Daniel Dennett is adamant that Darwin's theories demolish many traditional ideas—such as belief in God. Dennett playfully imagines his critics—there turn out to be rather a lot of these—demanding that Darwinism be kept on a tight leash: "Cede some or all of mod-ern biology to Darwin, perhaps, but hold the line there! Keep Darwinian thinking out of cosmology, out of psychology, out of human culture, out of ethics, politics and religion!"[31] For Dennett, Darwinism is a "universal acid" that corrodes the certainties of much traditional thought—especially religion.

Yet the attentive reader of this quote will notice a conspic-uous absence from the list of disciplines that Dennett suggests might benefit from Darwinian intervention: Dennett's own discipline of philosophy. If Darwinism is indeed the "universal acid" that Dennett proclaims it to be, it must be allowed to corrode his own ideas—not merely those of others.

It's easy to figure out why Dennett wanted to seal his philosophy in an acid-proof bubble: it relates to a disturbing question, fundamental to philosophy, that has recently received much attention: does natural selection select for truth or for survival? More than one evolutionary theorist has concluded that "natural selection does not care about truth; it cares only about reproductive success."[32] Is human reason hardwired for survival rather than for seeking truth? If so, what are its implications for the "pure reason" in which the New Atheism places so much trust?

For Hitchens, the precondition for human self-improvement is that we must be able to "transcend our prehistory."[33] If some of today's Darwinians are right, we may not be able to do this. Marx, Freud, Darwin, and others have forced us to confront the painful truth about the limits and biases of human reason. Their ideas may ultimately prove to be wrong, but they cannot be disregarded by the New Atheism. Might reason simply lock us into habits of thought and action we do not really understand? Might reason be shaped by hidden social and subconscious impulses so that what we believe to be pure reason is actually socially constructed and manipulated by our past history and subconscious motivations? Might natural human notions of goodness simply echo the demands of survival? These inconvenient questions are deeply controversial, yet they cannot be avoided by those who proclaim human reason as the supreme resource for life and thought.[34]

CONCLUSION

In this chapter, we've reflected on some aspects of the New Atheist appeal to reason in support of atheism. I'm quite reconciled to being told by New Atheists that my comments are predictable nonsense indicating how my mind has been messed up by a degenerate belief in God. Others, however, will easily see the force of the point being made—namely, that there are *multiple* valid conceptions of rationality. The rhetoric of the New Atheism would have the world divided into the rational and irrational. So what happens when we're forced to realize that there seem to be many ways of being rational? What becomes then of this simplistic dichotomist way of thinking?

I remember being taught Euclidean geometry at school in the early 1960s and learning all its definitions and axioms by heart. Unfortunately, nobody bothered to tell me that Euclid's approach represented just one way of doing geometry. It was an internally consistent system that many unwisely assumed to be the only rational system of its kind. It turned out that there were other, equally rational and consistent approaches, such as those of Nikolai Ivanovich Lobachevsky (1792–1856) or Bernhard Riemann (1826–66).[35] The casual and breezy New Atheist references to the rationality of godlessness and irrationality of belief in God merely invite the entirely proper question: "Which rationality do you mean?"[36] Religion may not conform to the New Atheism's dogmatic notions of rationality, but there are still plenty of rational alternatives. And belief in God turns out to be one of them.

Maybe that's why so many inside the movement now prefer to appeal to science instead—a trend we'll consider in the next chapter.

5

SCIENCE: A QUESTION OF PROOF

S cience is the great success story of human intellectual exploration. It's widely regarded as the securest and most reliable form of human knowledge, and it has gained this enviable reputation by the modesty of its ambition. Scientists know that they don't have to comment on everything— just what can be shown to be true by rigorous and testable investigation.

THE NATURE OF SCIENCE

Science seeks only to describe the forms and processes of the world; it declines to make observations on issues of meaning and value. And it's right to do so, for the cultural and intellectual authority of science depends critically upon its absolute neutrality in ethical, political, and religious debates. This point was made long ago when Darwin's great supporter Thomas H. Huxley (1825–95) famously declared that science "commits suicide when it adopts a creed."[1] Huxley was right. If science is hijacked by fundamentalists, whether religious or antireligious, its intellectual integrity is subverted and its cultural authority compromised.

In a sense, the natural sciences are the one remaining aspect of the Enlightenment project that has stood the test of time. The experimental method is universally valid and blind to the culture, race, religion, or gender of its researchers.[2] But while science may use rational methods of investigation, most notably the careful accumulation of evidence through observation and experiment, it does from time to time witness developments that are deeply counterintuitive and seem completely irrational (quantum theory providing many choice examples). Yet the question a scientist will ask is not, "Is this reasonable?" but, "What are the reasons for thinking this is true?"

There's an important point here about the limits of human rationality. The fact that the strangeness of the physical universe is not something we could possibly have predicted makes it clear that rationality is a matter of discovery rather than foresight. Science has learned to conform its thinking to the distinct and idiosyncratic nature of the universe rather than lay down in advance what form this ought to take.

Currently dominant approaches to the philosophy of science suggest that scientific advance takes place by identifying the "best explanation" of a set of observations.[3] A classic example illustrates this point well. In his *Principia Mathematica* (1687), Sir Isaac Newton (1643–1727) argued that the most satisfactory way of making sense of the motions of the moon and planets on the one hand, and of bodies falling to earth (such as his famous apple) on the other, was to propose the existence of something called *gravity*—an invisible force of attraction.[4] He was deeply suspicious of the idea, but it appeared to be the best explanation of observations of the world.

In other cases of scientific advance, the jury is still out. For example, two quite different approaches to quantum theory—the so-called Copenhagen school and the alternative developed by David Bohm—are equally elegant and, in theory at least, scientists haven't been able to decide which is right.[5] Similarly, in the recent debate about whether we need to think about a single universe or a "multiverse," the evidence is ambivalent and a case can be made for either view.[6]

Furthermore, science is a never-ending quest for the best understanding of things. The way things seem today will not be the way they're seen a century from now. (A hundred years ago, scientists thought that the universe had existed forever; that belief has now been replaced with the radically different notion that the universe came into being in a primordial fireball known as the Big Bang.[7]) The philosopher of science Michael Polanyi once shrewdly observed that scientists believed many things to be true but knew that some of those would eventually be shown to be wrong. The problem was that they didn't know which.

Today most scientists believe that Darwin's theory of natural selection is the best explanation of what we see in the world around us. But as Richard Dawkins rightly points out, Darwinism may eventually turn out to be wrong: "We must acknowledge the possibility that new facts may come to light which will force our successors of the twenty-first century to abandon Darwinism or modify it beyond recognition."[8] We need to be clear that a sensible recognition of the provisionality of scientific theories is not the same as resigning ourselves to a kind of relativism, each generation arbitrarily choosing what it wants to believe. Theoretical judgments are driven by evidence, and evidence accumulates over time, gradually leading to what the science historian Thomas Kuhn called "paradigm shifts"[9]—radical changes in the way we see things.

This point is not controversial in the philosophy of science, but my experience of debating the topic suggests that many ordinary people, especially within the New Atheism, have a rather simplistic take on science, believing that "science proves things." Let's explore this further.

DOES SCIENCE "PROVE" ITS THEORIES?

New Atheist Web sites tend to give the impression that scientific theories are based only on evidence. Religion, on the other hand, they posit, runs away from evidence. Richard Dawkins's argument that atheism is rational and scientific, while religion is irrational and superstitious, is clearly being picked up here. But just how reliable is it?

Dawkins often argues that there's no need for faith in science, in that the evidence for a correct conviction compels us to accept its truth. He first set out his views on this matter in *The Selfish Gene* in 1976 and has not changed his mind since.

> [Faith] is a state of mind that leads people to believe something—it doesn't matter what—in the total absence of supporting evidence. If there were good supporting evidence, then faith would be superfluous, for the evidence would compel us to believe it anyway.[10]

Though this seems clear and persuasive, it's actually an unsustainable view of the relation of evidence and belief in the natural sciences simply because it fails to make the critical distinction between the "total absence of supporting evidence" and the "absence of totally supporting evidence."

For example, consider the current debate within cosmology over whether the Big Bang gave rise to a single universe or a series of universes (the so-called multiverse).[11] I have many distinguished scientific colleagues who support the former approach and equally distinguished scientific colleagues who support the latter. Both are real options for thinking and informed scientists who make their decisions on the basis of their judgments of how best to interpret the evidence and who believe—but cannot prove—that their interpretation is correct. This process rather inconveniently doesn't fit at all with Dawkins's bold declaration that "if there were good supporting evidence, then faith would be superfluous, for the evidence would compel us to believe it anyway." Dawkins himself clearly believes in the multiverse theory, but the evidence for it just isn't good enough to compel him—or anyone else—to accept it. Science just isn't like that.[12]

In its rigorous sense, "proof" applies only to logic and mathematics. We can prove that $2 + 2 = 4$, just as we can prove that "the whole is greater than the part." Nevertheless, it's important to avoid confusing "provability" with "truth." As we noted earlier, the great mathematician Kurt Gödel famously proved that however many rules of inference we formulate, there will still be some valid inferences that are not covered by them. In other words, there are some statements that are true that we may not be able to show to be true.[13] The philosophical implications of this are considerable.[14]

In science, as we make a series of observations, we're forced to address these questions: "What must be true if we are to explain what is observed?" "What big picture of reality offers the best fit?" The American scientist and philosopher Charles S. Peirce (1839–1914) used the term *abduction* to refer to the way in which scientists generate theories that might offer the best explanation of things. The method is now more often referred to as "inference to the best explanation."

A classic example of this can be found in Charles Darwin's *Origin of Species* (1859), now widely seen as a landmark in scientific history. New Atheist Web sites often assert that Darwin proved his theories, contrasting this unfavorably with the "blind faith" of religion. Darwin himself knew otherwise. He believed that his theory of "natural selection" provided the most elegant and persuasive explanation of biological life forms—but he knew he couldn't prove it.[15] The problems were obvious.

To begin with, there was no "smoking gun"—no knockdown, unambiguous evidence that would conclusively and incontrovertibly compel people to accept his theory. Everything that was known about the natural world could be accommodated by rival theories, such as transformism.[16] Furthermore, there were serious scientific objections and difficulties to Darwin's theory that made it unacceptable to many scientists of his day.[17] The most significant of these was probably the problem of genetic dilution.[18] Darwin lacked a viable theory of genetics to explain how inherited characteristics were transmitted to subsequent generations.

Yet despite some formidable difficulties, Darwin believed that his theory was right and would one day be shown to be so. How, he asked, could a theory be wrong when it made so much sense of what he observed? Yes, there were loose ends everywhere and a large number of problems. But his core idea seemed to him to be correct—even though it couldn't be proved.

> A crowd of difficulties will have occurred to the reader. Some of them are so grave that to this day I can never reflect on them without being staggered; but, to the best of my judgment, the greater number are only apparent, and those that are real are not, I think, fatal to my theory.[19]

So does science *prove* its theories? There are certainly some things that science (as opposed to logic and mathematics) can prove and has proved—that the chemical formula for water is H_2O, for example, or that the average distance of the moon from the earth is about 384,500 kilometers. But these are basically facts about our world. The big scientific questions concern notions about the origins of the universe, the nature of force and matter, and perhaps the biggest question of all: is there a Grand Unified Theory that can explain everything? We can give to these questions good answers that we believe can be justified from the best evidence at our disposal. But we can't give a *final* answer because we know that what scientists believe today may not be what scientists believe in the future. No wonder standard scientific textbooks rightly emphasize that "science rests on faith."[20]

Most people don't have a problem with this. Faith is just part of human life and plays an important role in science as it does everywhere else. However, the New Atheism tends to have an aversion to the word, believing that "faith" denotes some kind of intellectual perversity reserved for deluded religious fools. Faith, we're told, is invariably *blind* faith. Quite clearly it's not: belief is just a normal human way of making sense of a complex world. As the philosopher Julia Kristeva observed, "Whether I belong to a religion, whether I be agnostic or atheist, when I say 'I believe,' I mean 'I hold as true.'"[21]

In the end, science is about giving us reasons for believing that certain things are true, while at the same time insisting that we realize that future generations may rightly want to challenge these beliefs. That's why science is so successful: it's willing to change its mind in response to new evidence. But what about things that lie beyond the scientific method?

The Limits of Science

The natural sciences are empirical in their approach—in other words, they rely on the application of observation and experiment in investigating the world. Yet empiricism refuses, as a matter of principle, to speculate about any realities beyond the observable world. Bas van Fraassen, a leading philosopher of science, makes this point clearly:

> To be an empiricist is to withhold belief in anything that goes beyond the actual, observable phenomena, and to recognize no objective modality in nature. To develop an empiricist account of science is to depict it as involving a search for truth only about the empirical world, about what is actual and observable . . . it must invoke throughout a resolute rejection of the demand for an explanation of the regularities in the observable course of nature by means of truths concerning a reality beyond what is actual and observable.[22]

This emphasis on what's "actual and observable" gives the sciences their distinct identity. It also defines their limits.

In arguments with zealous New Atheist foot soldiers—most of whom, I say with some regret, seem to know astonishingly little about the history and philosophy of science—I regularly find that one of the easiest ways to make them furious is to tell them that science can't answer some of life's great questions. I'm accused of all sorts of things when I do this, usually of peddling "typical religious obscurantism" or spouting "antiscientific nonsense." As the writings of Richard Dawkins carry the status of Holy Writ for many of these very earnest people, I take pleasure in pointing out how Dawkins himself correctly emphasizes the moral limits of science: "science has no methods for deciding what is ethical."[23] This does, I have to say, throw them into some confusion. They often don't know very much about Richard Dawkins either.

The clumsy word *scientism*—often glossed as "scientific imperialism"[24]—is now used to refer to the view that science can solve all our problems, explain human nature, or tell us what's morally good.[25] It claims that all that's known or can be known is capable of verification or falsification using the scientific method. Anything that cannot be verified or falsified in this manner is to be regarded as at best mere private opinion or belief and at worst delusion or fantasy. Very few natural scientists embrace scientific imperialism, to my knowledge. It appears to appeal to a handful of philosophers on the one hand and a much larger cohort of adherents of popular "scientific atheism" on the other.

Two areas of thought that clearly lie beyond the legitimate scope of the natural sciences are the nonempirical notions of *value* and *meaning*. These cannot be read off the world or measured as if they were constants of nature. As the philosopher Hilary Putnam rightly notes, while there's such a thing as "correctness in ethics," it's important not to model our ethical thinking "on the ways in which we get things right in physics."[26] It's been known since the eighteenth century that there are formidable intellectual obstacles in the way of anyone wanting to argue that science can generate moral values, most notably the impossibility of arguing from observed facts to moral values.

The New Atheist celebrity Sam Harris tries to argue otherwise in his most recent book, *The Moral Landscape*.[27] Moral values are about promoting human well-being. Since science tells about what promotes well-being, it can determine moral values. There's no need for God or religion. Science can tell us what's right. So what of the massive problems that philosophers know are associated with this kind of approach?[28] Harris deals with these by kicking them into the long grass, hoping that nobody who knows anything about the debate will notice his failure to engage with these problems.[29] In the interests of reaching a "wider audience," Harris avoids precisely the serious philosophical discussion that his position demands. The outcome is a lightweight and seriously deficient view of the foundations of morality.

My atheist colleagues had hoped that Harris would stop

ranting against religion and do some serious positive thinking instead. The New Atheism, in their view, desperately needed to show that it could do something other than rage against faith. Unfortunately, it looks as though Harris just can't break the habit. A whole chapter is needlessly given over to antireligious polemic when it should have been used to deal with precisely the objections to his own position that Harris so badly needed to engage. The New Atheism is great at antireligious rhetoric, but it's yet to show that it can put forward a positive and defensible alternative to faith-based values.

Religion engages with questions that lie beyond the scope of the scientific method—such as the existence of God, the meaning of life, and the nature of values. These are all open to rational debate; it's very doubtful whether they're open to scientific analysis in that they're not empirical notions. I find myself in broad agreement with the conclusions of Sir Peter Medawar (1915–97), who won the Nobel Prize in medicine for his work on immunology. Medawar draws a distinction between "transcendent" questions, which he thought were best left to religion and metaphysics, and questions about the organization and structure of the material universe. Medawar insists that it's "very likely" that there are limits to science, given "the existence of questions that science cannot answer, and that no conceivable advance of science would empower it to answer."[30] Medawar makes it explicitly clear that he has in mind questions such as, "What are we all here for?" "What's the point of living?" These are real questions, and we're right to seek answers to them. But science—if applied legitimately—isn't going to help. We need to look elsewhere.

The New Atheism sees science as some kind of one-way intellectual superhighway to atheism. It's not. Science can be made to resonate with atheism just as it can be made to resonate with Christian belief. It may certainly challenge some religious approaches that claim to offer a "scientific" view of things. But in and of itself science is theistically neutral—unless it abandons the scientific method and strays into the more speculative world of metaphysics.

WARFARE: SCIENCE AS THE ENEMY OF RELIGION

From what's been said, it seems that God lies outside the scope of the scientific method. In one sense science has nothing legitimate to say about God. As the great Harvard evolutionary biologist Stephen Jay Gould (1941–2002) rightly remarked, "Science simply cannot (by its legitimate methods) adjudicate the issue of God's possible superintendence of nature. We neither affirm nor deny it; we simply can't comment on it as scientists."[31] In fact, Dawkins and other New Atheists comment rather a lot on this matter, but perhaps that's because they speak here primarily as a militant atheists rather than scientists.

While scholarship has shown that the origins of "scientific atheism" as a faith tradition can be traced back to the eighteenth century,[32] the New Atheism has given it a new importance and profile through its appeal to the natural sciences in defense of its atheist outlook. In the New Atheist worldview, as we've seen, science is about what can be proved to be true, whereas religion is about running away from the facts and seeking consolation in outdated, discredited, and immoral Bronze Age myths.

For example, Christopher Hitchens regularly asserts that people believed the earth was flat because of religious dogma. It's a puzzling assertion as historical scholarship long ago showed that virtually every Christian scholar of the Middle Ages acknowledged the sphericity of the earth.[33] Some of them were even able to calculate its approximate circumference. The urban myth that religion demanded a flat earth is now known to have developed in the late nineteenth century, and it's really time to give it up!

It's not unreasonable to argue that the New Atheism does more than simply reflect the cultural stereotype of the "warfare" of science and religion; it actually depends upon it for its plausibility. The origins of this idea—often referred to as the "conflict thesis" in scholarly works—lies in the massive social shifts that took place in Victorian England. In the early part of the nineteenth century, most English scientists were ordained clergy of the Church of England who saw no tension between their faith and the scientific method. With the passing of time, it became increasingly important for scientists to assert their independence of the church—or any other institution. This led to a significant shift in the dynamics of cultural power as scientists began to wrest cultural and professional authority from their clerical counterparts in shaping intellectual inquiry and values.[34]

The perception that science and religion were at war with each other was not, as some New Atheist writers seem to think, the result of the Darwinian debates. It actually arose later in the nineteenth century through highly polemical popular works such as John Draper's *History of the Conflict Between Religion and Science* (1874) and Andrew White's *History of the Warfare of Science with Theology* (1896). Through shrewd manipulation of the historical evidence, these passionate books portrayed noble, honest, objective, and heroic scientists as victims struggling to defend the truth against odious, manipulative, and repressive Catholic clergy.

These two works, today remembered as much for their ideological stridency as their historical inaccuracy, had a deep impact on atheist thinking. Bertrand Russell, for example, draws uncritically on both sources in his *History of Western Philosophy*. Despite (or perhaps on account of?) their lightweight and superficial reading of history, they established the popular stereotype of the warfare of science and religion that persists to this day, largely through uncritical repetition in the media.

The "warfare" model underlay the appeal to science as a core component of the Soviet Union's attempt to impose its official atheism on an unwilling and unpersuaded public. In my study I have a photograph of the library of the Timiriazev Scientific Research Institute for the Study and Propaganda of the Scientific Foundations of Dialectical Materialism,[35] taken around the year 1931. This institute, originally dedicated to biological research, became part of the spearhead of the Soviet Union's attempt to eliminate religion by an appeal to science. On the library wall a massive banner reads, "The front line of the battle against religion!"

In the end Stalin's approach just didn't work. Belief in God was still rampant in the Soviet Union when Stalin died in 1953, forcing the Communist Party to begin an aggressive program of indoctrination the following year, decreeing that "the teaching of school subjects (history, literature, natural sciences, physics, chemistry, etc.) should be saturated with atheism."[36] Soviet school textbooks repeatedly asserted the malevolence of religion through breezy slogans such as "Religion is a fanatical and perverse reflection of the world" or "Religion has become the means of the spiritual enslavement of the masses." Yet all that this socially manipulative program of using science as a weapon against religion achieved was to lay the foundations for the massive rebirth of belief in God after the collapse of the Soviet Union in the 1990s.

For the record, historians of science are generally agreed to have shown during the 1970s that the "conflict thesis" was historically untenable.[37] The myths on which it depended so critically—especially in popular atheist propaganda—have been comprehensively dismantled,[38] and in recent decades popular culture has become increasingly willing to engage with the messier complexities of history and culture instead of reducing them to mindless slogans and stereotypes. Everyone knows that *science* and *religion* are shorthand terms for enormously complex and diverse beliefs, practices, and communities. Crass generalizations are intrinsically dangerous here.

Earlier I noted how the New Atheism disregards the huge body of scholarly literature concerning the nature and impact of religion. Unfortunately, the same is true of the history and philosophy of science. Why can't the New Atheism take this literature seriously? To its critics it's at least a century out of date with its reading.

Yes there are tensions—often serious—between some religious thinkers and some scientists. There always have been and always will be. But we're also seeing synergies, resonances, and the possibility of dialogue and mutual enrichment—perhaps more so today than ever before. The New Atheism is angered and exasperated by the growing number of scientists interested in metaphysical and religious questions, frequently portraying such people in rather hysterical terms as collaborating with the enemy.[39] But that's only how it looks if you're psychologically fixated on the historically obsolete "warfare" model. It's time to move on and leave these discredited certainties of the past behind.

And there are signs that this is happening. In 2008, Richard Dawkins retired as professor of the public understanding of science at Oxford University. His militant atheism had made this position controversial, linking the affirmation of science with the ridicule of religion. He was succeeded by the distinguished mathematician Marcus du Sautoy. Journalists flocked to interview him, chiefly interested in one question: would he follow in Dawkins's footsteps and make this chair a personal pulpit for atheism? Du Sautoy's answer was crisp and convincing. Though he was an atheist himself, he would "absolutely not" be indulging in antireligious polemic. His job was to promote science, and he looked forward to doing that with enthusiasm.[40]

These comments provoked anger from some on the Dawkins Web site.[41] What kind of scientist was this? Why had he not given Dawkins the honor due to him? If du Sautoy was a real scientist, he'd be rubbishing religion! What a ridiculous choice for this chair! One commenter noted, "If he's going to promote the public understanding of science he has to confront the daily challenges of religion to rationality." Just as well Dawkins was still around to tell the truth about science, since this newcomer was clearly not up to the job. Yet du Sautoy's approach represents an important step back to normality. Maybe there's hope that civilized conversation will at last take the place of confrontation and ridicule in this important field.

The Twentieth Century: The Seismic Shift

The relation of science and faith changed decisively in the later twentieth century. Although New Atheist propagandists regularly declare that scientific advance and progress have eroded the case for belief in God, the facts are otherwise.

The first decades of the twentieth century were dominated by a scientific belief in the eternity of the universe. It had always existed. Religious language about "creation" was seen as mythological nonsense, incompatible with cutting-edge scientific knowledge.

This belief played an important role in the great 1948 debate between two leading British philosophers—the atheist Bertrand Russell (1872–1970) and the Christian Frederick

Copleston (1907–90)—that's widely regarded as a classic exploration of the issues.[42] Russell thought this scientific consensus was more than sufficient to put paid to the whole God question once and for all. The universe is just there, and there's no good reason to think about what brought it into being.

But things have changed since 1948. During the 1960s, it became increasingly clear that the universe had an origin— the Big Bang.[43] Though this idea was met with fierce resistance by some atheist scientists of the day, such as the astrophysicist Fred Hoyle, who was worried that it sounded "religious," happily this prejudice was overwhelmed by the evidence in its favor. And it's an undeniable fact that the new understanding of the origins of the universe resonates strongly with the Christian doctrine of creation.

A replay of the Russell–Copleston debate was staged in 1998 to mark its fiftieth anniversary. It featured two leading philosophers, the Christian William Lane Craig and the (then) atheist Anthony Flew.[44] Craig, the philosopher who many now regard as the natural successor to Copleston, developed the following line of argument:

Major premise: whatever begins to exist has a cause.
Minor premise: the universe began to exist.
Conclusion: therefore the universe has a cause.

Note that, unusually, the minor premise, which would have been comprehensively rejected in 1948, is now accepted by virtually every scientist as of possibly even greater importance than the major. Flew experienced considerable difficulty at this point and was unable to deploy the strategies used by earlier generations of atheist apologists with any plausibility. For several years before his death in 2010, Flew explicitly affirmed his belief in a God. He had moved away from his earlier atheism, taking up a position I would characterize as a form of deism.[45]

This fundamental shift in the scientific consensus has changed the tone of the debate about God. Also important is the growing realization that the universe came into being "fine-tuned" for life.[46] The fundamental constants of nature seem to be fixed at certain values that make our existence possible. Fred Hoyle was one of the first to appreciate this phenomenon and its obvious theistic interpretation. It is, he wrote, as if "a superintellect has monkeyed with physics, as well as with chemistry and biology, and that there are no blind forces worth speaking about in nature."[47]

Fine-tuning proves nothing, but it is deeply suggestive. It resonates strongly with the Christian way of thinking.[48] The cosmology of the early twenty-first century is much more sympathetic to Christian belief than that of a century ago.

SCIENCE AND REASON:
SOME CONCLUDING THOUGHTS

So where do these reflections on reason and science leave us? Both have much to say, yet we can still ask good and meaningful questions that neither reason nor science can answer. And we're right to look elsewhere when they fail to provide adequate responses. If it is to remain true to the criteria by which it demands that others should be judged, the New Atheism must restrict itself to the domain of the rationally and scientifically verified and verifiable. The New Atheism's search for liberation from what it terms *superstition* seems to have ended up confining humanity within a self-made and self-imposed cage.

But is this domain existentially and morally habitable? It may have been thought so back in the eighteenth century. Yet as Sir Isaiah Berlin noted, the dominant mood in Western culture from the late nineteenth century onward has been "the rejection of reason and order as being prison houses of the spirit."[49] To limit oneself to what reason and science can prove is merely to skim the surface of reality and fail to discover the hidden depths beneath. The rise of fantasy writings—such as fairy tales in the Victorian era[50] and their later development in J. R. R. Tolkien and C. S. Lewis—is an important reflection of this loss of confidence in the existential adequacy of scientific rationalism.

In late 2007, Richard Dawkins and the Oxford mathematician John Lennox met in Alabama for an interesting and widely discussed debate in which most of the questions arising from the New Atheism were explored, especially those relating to science and faith.[51] The Christian online community had no doubts about the outcome: Lennox won.

Many in the New Atheist virtual community also reluctantly drew that same conclusion. They were disturbed by Lennox's argumentative prowess and clearly in shock that the core ideas of the New Atheism had been so successfully challenged on rational and scientific grounds. But more significantly, some began to realize that reason and science might actually point toward God rather than toward atheism. What New Atheist foot soldiers had regarded as reliable allies might turn out to be traitors. The following deeply frustrated comment, posted on Richard Dawkins's Web site, is representative of the tone of that reaction:

> Why is everyone surprised that these debates all end the same way[?] Why, why would we expect something better from the religionists? I'm beginning to believe the best we can do is to just shout at them, "You're stupid, you're idiots, you're morons!!" It is probably as effective as using reason and logic. Reason and logic are anathema to these people. I'm going to yell at them.[52]

This commenter was clearly shocked that reason and science not only failed to persuade Lennox but seemed to point toward theism. So what could be done? Best just to yell at Lennox and others and tell them they're morons. Shout them down if you can't win the argument. And that, in the view of many critical observers, is precisely the form that much New Atheist polemic now takes. Unfortunately, many contributors to New Atheist Web sites seem to think that loud and rude insults trump evidence-based arguments. I'm not sure whether that tells us something about the intellectual weakness of the New Atheism or about the state of contemporary Western culture.

There are clear signs of a dawning realization of this point within the New Atheist community. While their cheerleaders urge them to trust reason and science, insisting that they offer an incorrigible and irrefutable foundation for atheism, freethinkers within the movement are coming to realize that their beliefs are simplistic—where they once thought they were plain simple.

PART THREE

WHERE DOES THE NEW ATHEISM GO FROM HERE?

6

WHERE IS THE NEW ATHEISM NOW?

The New Atheism burst onto the scene in 2006, brimful of energy and passion. Its infectious self-confidence and punchy sound bites captivated many in the media. The future, many declared, was Bright. Religion would not survive the shock of the New Atheism.

But how do things look now?

In May 2010, Christopher Hitchens debated the Christian philosopher John Haldane at Oxford University. The topic—the place of secularism and religion in public life—was genuinely interesting. What insights would Hitchens bring to this important matter?

Remarkably few, as it turned out. Hitchens simply repeated his habitual tirades against religion like a stand-up comic delivering an overfamiliar spiel. The high point of a rather dull evening, according to Oxford's student newspaper, was Hitchens's faintly amusing dismissal of the archbishop of Canterbury, Rowan Williams—who was not present—as a "sheep-faced loon."[1] Even that pearl turned out to have been recycled, Hitchens having used this phrase several times before to dismiss clerics who'd crossed his path.[2] It might reasonably be wondered, to paraphrase the English playwright Richard Sheridan, whether Hitchens is now relying on his memory for his jokes and his imagination for his facts.[3]

The truth is that Hitchens's archiepiscopal insult doesn't detract from the archbishop of Canterbury's fundamental criticism of the New Atheism—namely, that it simply attacks easy and lazy caricatures or degenerate forms of religion, ignoring the mainstream reality; and more important, that it fails to articulate a positive and compelling approach of its own.

THE RISE OF SKEPTICISM ABOUT THE NEW ATHEISM

Atheist blogs now regularly feature agonized reflections on the failure of the movement to gain the intellectual high ground. Appeals to reason and science have failed to score anything even remotely approaching knockout blows against belief in God. To the intense irritation of New Atheist apologists, their Christian opponents regularly appeal to both in their critique of atheism and in their proclamation of the rationality and relevance of the Christian faith. Recently, more books than ever have been published asserting the intrinsic rationality of Christian belief. It's not comfortable for New Atheist foot soldiers to have their weapons used so effectively against them.

Even worse, society at large has not bought into the movement's analysis of the "pathological" role of religion. For the New Atheists it's obvious that religious extremism was behind 9/11. So why do opinion makers ignore this? Why did Barack Obama *praise* faith in his 2008 election campaign instead of rubbishing it? It's delusional!

And it's not just in the United States that things are going wrong. When the pope visited the United Kingdom in September 2010, Richard Dawkins and Christopher Hitchens demanded that he be arrested for "crimes against humanity."[4] Mass protests were promised against him. In the end, the pope was not arrested. The enthusiastic crowds who flocked to welcome him vastly outnumbered those who gathered to protest. The public saw not a "leering old villain in a frock"[5] but a frail, intelligent, and perceptive person with a message worth listening to. The pope's sensitive and reflective addresses were well received, especially by the British political establishment. As a result, the New Atheism was left exposed—not simply as numerically weak but as culturally isolated. After the visit ended, the UK's most secular newspaper, the *Independent*, even published an article entitled "Pope Benedict . . . an Apology."[6]

When Reason Fails: The New Atheist Art of Ridicule

Having been failed by reason and science, the New Atheism is now, as the humanist Brian Epstein has pointed out with obvious exasperation, reduced to "seek[ing] to shame and embarrass people away from religion, browbeating them about the stupidity of belief in a bellicose god" (quoted more fully in chapter 2). Things hit rock-bottom on September 30, 2009. This was the date chosen by the Center for Inquiry—which promotes itself as the intellectual powerhouse of American secularism and has close links to the New Atheism—to be the first ever "Blasphemy Day." The idea was to use freedom of speech to insult religions and religious people. The Center organized an art exhibition to mark this momentous event and included in the works exhibited a piece entitled *Jesus Paints His Nails*. It depicted a rather effeminate Jesus applying polish to the nails fixing his hands to the cross.

The CEO of the Center for Inquiry, Ronald A. Lindsay, defended this and the other exhibits as "thoughtful, incisive and concise critiques of religion."[7] His was something of a lone supportive voice. Other atheists were shocked. Stuart Jordan, an advisor to the Center, believed the aggressive approach of the exhibition would backfire against atheism. What was the point in insulting people for their beliefs? He wouldn't want *Jesus Paints His Nails* on his walls.

For Jordan, this episode was an indication of bitter debate within the American atheist movement as a whole over its future direction. For further clarification, it's well worth reflecting on the sad but instructive tale of Paul Kurtz.

Paul Kurtz (born 1925) is one of the United States' most prominent secular humanists,[8] seen by many as the godfather of the New Atheism. Kurtz was instrumental in reshaping American humanism in a specifically secular direction during the late 1970s and early 1980s, largely by suppressing its historic religious origins and continuing religious associations and commitments. The original American "Humanist Manifesto" (1933) made specific approving reference to religious humanism. Kurtz vigorously advocated more secular forms of humanism and formed the Council for Secular Humanism to lobby for a change in direction of the American Humanist Association. He was one of the two primary authors of "Humanist Manifesto II" (1973), setting out a vision for a form of humanism that distanced itself from traditional religious possibilities and affirmations.[9] He founded the Center for Inquiry in 1991 to promote this form of humanism.

So how, you might ask, could someone as canny as Paul

Kurtz allow a public relations debacle like Blasphemy Day to take place? The simple answer is that he didn't. The Center for Inquiry, which had lurched toward increasing militancy earlier in 2009, threw him out three months prior to September 30. Kurtz's own account of this development merits reading, especially in the light of the Center's bland statement that he had "resigned":

> I was unceremoniously ousted as Chairman of the Center for Inquiry/Transnational on June 1, 2009. It is totally untruthful to state that I was not. The effort by the CEO [Ronald A. Lindsay] to cover up this deed offends any sense of fairness and I do not wish to be party to that deception. It was a palace coup clear and simple by those who wish to seize immediate power.[10]

Kurtz was appalled by the aggressive new direction that was then taken by his organization under its new leadership. The viciousness of this New Atheism, he declared, was likely to set the cause of atheism back. "Angry atheism does not work!"[11] The New Atheism would just come to be seen as a form of intolerant fundamentalism that ridiculed its opponents rather than seeking to understand and engage them. This "atheist fundamentalism" is, Kurtz suggested, fundamentally "mean-spirited."

Some years ago I used the phrase "atheist fundamentalism"

to refer to the specific form of atheism I found in the recent writings of Richard Dawkins. It's interesting to see a leading atheist explicitly and approvingly employing it against the obvious excesses of the New Atheism. Let me make it clear that I would not dream of applying this phrase to the academically thoughtful and culturally respectful atheism of writers such as Iris Murdoch or the studied neutrality of an "atheism of indifference." But it's right on target to describe the dogmatic intolerance of the New Atheism, which resembles the nastier forms of religious fundamentalism at these points.

Kurtz profoundly hoped that this new "aggressive and militant phase" in the history of atheism would fizzle out before it inflicted lasting damage on the movement. This "dogmatic attitude," he declared, "holds that *this and only this is true* and that anyone who deviates from it is a fool."[12] It was no wonder, he suggested, that the New Atheism had lost public sympathy and credibility:

> Most atheists that I know are decent and compassionate folk. What I object to are the militant atheists who are narrow-minded about religious persons and will have nothing to do with agnostics, skeptics, or those who are indifferent to religion, dismissing them as cowardly.[13]

For Kurtz, the viciousness of the New Atheism was damaging the public face of atheism. And it was a self-inflicted wound, not one meted out by its critics. No wonder media reports since then speak openly of a "schism" or "rift" within the secular humanist movement.

Though the debates arising from the New Atheism continue to have some popular appeal, it seems clear that they've lost a great deal of their intellectual traction. Will the movement be like the pseudoscientific notion of the "meme"—such a core element of Dawkins's and Dennett's defense of atheism—"a short-lived fad whose effect has been to obscure more than it has been to enlighten" (quoted more fully in chapter 1)? It will be interesting to see.

7

GOD WON'T GO AWAY:
BEYOND THE NEW ATHEISM

hristopher Hitchens and I disagree on many things.
I regard Mother Teresa of Calcutta (1910–97) as a
remarkable woman who served the poor with a love
and dedication I could never imitate but would love to emu-
late. As we saw in chapter 2, Hitchens considers her a "fraud"
who made life worse for "millions of people."[1] What a pity,
he remarked, that there was no hell for her to go to. But at
least we agree on some things. One is that religion is not going
to disappear. As Hitchens remarks, with an obvious sense of
exasperation, it is "ineradicable."[2]

He's right. Things have changed since the 1960s, when I
was growing up. The received wisdom of that bygone age was
that religion was on its way out, both at the social and personal
level. Back then, "the most illustrious figures in sociology,

anthropology and psychology" were unanimously of the view that they "would live to see the dawn of a new era in which, to paraphrase Freud, the infantile illusions of religion would be outgrown."[3] A generation later, this judgment can no longer be sustained. Faith is back in public life. Serious political debate in Western Europe—widely regarded as the most secular geopolitical region in the world—now increasingly concerns how best to work with faith groups and use faith to generate social cohesion and consolidate social capital.[4]

Why is faith still alive and well, despite routine predictions of its demise and ritual denunciations of its perniciousness? The answer Hitchens offers—following eighteenth-century precedents[5]—is that human beings are intrinsically superstitious. They need to be weaned off such nonsense. Natural beliefs are wrong. They need to be corrected in the light of science and reason. Dawkins and Dennett are rather more up-to-date in their analysis, arguing that religion is essentially a by-product of the evolutionary process.[6]

There are, however, problems with the arguments leading to this conclusion, as well as in assessing its possible implications. Suppose it could be shown that human beings possess an evolutionary adaptation to seek the truth. Would this invalidate the quest for truth? Would people stop searching for truth because it is suggested that our evolutionary history predisposes us to do so? I hardly think so.

It's not my intention to argue the case for the Christian faith in this short volume,[7] yet I can hardly fail to point out that the common Christian understanding of human nature over the last two thousand years is that we possess, and are meant to possess, a homing instinct for God.[8] To use an image from the Renaissance poet Francis Quarles (1592–1644), our soul is like an iron needle drawn to the magnetic pole of God. God can no more be eliminated from human life than our yearning for justice or our deep desire to make this world a better place. We have a homing instinct precisely because there's a home for us to return to. That's one of the great themes of the New Testament. We are created with an inbuilt yearning for God, famously expressed in the prayer of Augustine of Hippo (354–430): "You have made us for yourself, and our heart is restless until it finds its rest in you." One of the reasons Christianity makes such a powerful appeal to humanity is its ability to make sense of our experience.

Richard Dawkins and Daniel Dennett spend pages of their weighty New Atheist tomes speculating about why human beings are preconditioned to believe in God, generally passing off speculation as though it were the solid findings of science. Yet Dawkins and Dennett rather miss the point here. They seem to think that they discredit Christianity by offering "scientific" explanations for religious belief. But while they may clarify the mechanisms by which we long for God, yearn to do good, eliminate poverty, or defend the oppressed, such "explanations" neither explain away nor invalidate these deep instincts. They're part of who we are as human beings and serve to disclose the true possibilities that lie within us—and beyond us.

I cannot pursue this matter further here. Christian beliefs, like those of the New Atheism or any other worldview, ultimately lie beyond final rational proof. But they're clearly of no small importance in understanding the current worldwide resurgence of interest in faith and its implications for more aggressive forms of secularism. The political philosopher Charles Taylor concluded his recent magisterial analysis of the emergence of a "secular age" with an assertion that religion will not and cannot disappear because of the distinctive characteristics of human nature—above all, what the French philosopher and political historian Chantal Millon-Delsol calls a "*désir d'éternité,*" or "desire for eternity."[9] There's something about human nature that makes us want to reach out beyond rational and empirical limits, questing for meaning and significance.

For Taylor the fundamental characteristics of human nature are such that there can really never be a totally "secular" outlook.[10] Religious beliefs and practices work with the grain of human nature. No account of human nature or aspirations can ignore this point—not even the New Atheism, which so clearly fails to address the obvious fact that most people experience religion as liberating and supportive.

The ironic fact is that New Atheist anger at the persistence of faith has inadvertently stirred huge interest in the whole God question. It's made people want to reflect on the other side of the story . . .

I'd just finished giving a lecture in London early in 2010. A young man came up afterward and asked me to sign a copy of my textbook *Christian Theology: An Introduction*. I asked him what had led him to study theology. He told me that he'd read Richard Dawkins's *The God Delusion* a year or so earlier and it seemed so unfair and one-sided that he felt he needed to hear the other side. So he started going to church. After a while he found he could not sustain his faith in the parody when confronted with the real thing. He converted to Christianity— joyfully and decisively. "Without Dawkins," he told me, "I would never have given God a second thought."

As I signed the book, the young man told me he had a theological question for me. Since *The God Delusion* had been instrumental in his conversion, should he thank God for Richard Dawkins in his prayers?

I'm still thinking about that one.

FURTHER READING

Classic Statements of the New Atheism

Dawkins, Richard. *The God Delusion*. London: Bantam, 2006.

Dennett, Daniel C. *Breaking the Spell: Religion as a Natural Phenomenon*. New York: Viking Penguin, 2006.

Harris, Sam. *The End of Faith: Religion, Terror, and the Future of Reason*. New York: W. W. Norton, 2004.

———. *Letter to a Christian Nation*. New York: Knopf, 2006.

Hitchens, Christopher. *God Is Not Great: How Religion Poisons Everything*. New York: Twelve, 2007.

Other Atheist Works of Interest,
Not Necessarily Advocating the New Atheism

Blackford, Russell, ed. *50 Voices of Disbelief: Why We Are Atheists*. Malden, MA: Wiley-Blackwell, 2009.

Kurtz, Paul W. *Multi-Secularism: A New Agenda*. Piscataway, NJ: Transaction Publishers, 2010.

Loftus, John W. *The Christian Delusion: Why Faith Fails*. Amherst, NY: Prometheus Books, 2010.

Mills, David. *Atheist Universe: The Thinking Person's Answer to Christian Fundamentalism*. Berkeley, CA: Ulysses Press, 2006.

Onfray, Michel. *Atheist Manifesto: The Case Against Christianity, Judaism, and Islam*. New York: Arcade, 2007.

Ray, Daniel W. *The God Virus: How Religion Infects Our Lives and Culture*. Bonner Springs, KS: IPC Press, 2009.

Stenger, Victor J. *God: The Failed Hypothesis: How Science Shows That God Does Not Exist*. Amherst, NY: Prometheus Books, 2008.

———. *The New Atheism: Taking a Stand for Science and Reason*. Amherst, NY: Prometheus Books, 2009.

Criticisms of and Responses to the New Atheism, Reflecting Both Christian and Secular Perspectives

Armstrong, Karen. *The Case for God*. New York: Knopf, 2009.

Beattie, Tina. *The New Atheists: The Twilight of Reason and the War on Religion*. London: Darton, Longman & Todd, 2007.

Berlinski, David. *The Devil's Delusion: Atheism and Its Scientific Pretensions*. New York: Basic Books, 2009.

Cavanaugh, William T. *The Myth of Religious Violence*. Oxford: Oxford University Press, 2009.

Cornwell, John. *Darwin's Angel: A Seraphic Response to the God Delusion*. London: Profile Books, 2007.

Craig, William Lane and Chad V. Meister, eds. *God Is Great, God Is Good: Why Believing in God Is Reasonable and Responsible*. Downers Grove, IL: InterVarsity, 2009.

Crean, Thomas. *God Is No Delusion: A Refutation of Richard Dawkins*. San Francisco: Ignatius Press, 2007.

D'Souza, Dinesh. *What's So Great About Christianity*. Washington, DC: Regnery, 2007.

Eagleton, Terry. *Reason, Faith, and Revolution: Reflections on the God Debate*. New Haven, CT: Yale University Press, 2009.

Fergusson, David. *Faith and Its Critics: A Conversation*. Oxford: Oxford University Press, 2009.

Hahn, Scott. *Answering the New Atheism: Dismantling Dawkins' Case Against God*. Steubenville, OH: Emmaus Road, 2008.

Hart, David Bentley. *Atheist Delusions: The Christian Revolution and Its Fashionable Enemies*. New Haven, CT: Yale University Press, 2009.

Haught, John F. *God and the New Atheism: A Critical Response to Dawkins, Harris, and Hitchens*. Louisville, KY: Westminster John Knox Press, 2008.

Keller, Timothy J. *The Reason for God: Belief in an Age of Skepticism*. New York: Dutton, 2008.

Lennox, John. *God's Undertaker: Has Science Buried God?* Oxford: Lion, 2007.

Markham, Ian S. *Against Atheism: Why Dawkins, Hitchens, and Harris Are Fundamentally Wrong*. Oxford: Blackwell, 2010.

McGrath, Alister E. and Joanna Collicutt McGrath. *The Dawkins Delusion? Atheist Fundamentalism and the Denial of the Divine*. London: SPCK, 2007.

McGrath, Alister E. *Surprised by Meaning: Science, Faith, and How We Make Sense of Things*. Louisville, KY: Westminster John Knox Press, 2011.

Mohler, R. Albert. *Atheism Remix: A Christian Confronts the New Atheists*. Wheaton, IL: Crossway Books, 2008.

Myers, David G. *A Friendly Letter to Skeptics and Atheists: Musings on Why God Is Good and Faith Isn't Evil*. San Francisco, CA: Jossey-Bass, 2008.

Novak, Michael. *No One Sees God: The Dark Night of Atheists and Believers.* New York: Doubleday, 2008.

Robertson, David. *The Dawkins Letters: Challenging Atheist Myths.* Ross-shire, Scotland: Christian Focus, 2007.

Stewart, Robert B. *The Future of Atheism: Alister McGrath and Daniel Dennett in Dialogue.* Minneapolis: Fortress Press, 2008.

Ward, Keith. *Why There Almost Certainly Is a God: Doubting Dawkins.* Oxford: Lion Hudson, 2008.

Wright, N.T. *Simply Christian: Why Christianity Makes Sense.* San Francisco: HarperOne, 2006.

Zacharias, Ravi K. *The End of Reason: A Response to the New Atheists.* Grand Rapids, MI: Zondervan, 2008.

NOTES

Introduction

1. The capitalized term *New Atheism* is used throughout to refer specifically to the movement now known by this name, rather than the more general and imprecise idea of "more recent forms of atheism."
2. Richard Dawkins, "Religion's Misguided Missiles," *Guardian*, 15 September 2001.
3. "In God's Name: A Special Report on Religion and Public Life," *Economist*, 3 November 2007. For an expansion of these views by *Economist* writers, see John Micklethwait and Adrian Wooldridge, *God Is Back: How the Global Revival of Faith Is Changing the World* (New York: Penguin Press, 2009).

1. The New Atheism: How It All Started

1. Sam Harris, *The End of Faith: Religion, Terror, and the Future of Reason* (New York: W. W. Norton & Company, 2004).
2. Richard Dawkins, *The God Delusion* (London: Bantam, 2006).
3. Daniel Dennett, *Breaking the Spell: Religion as a Natural Phenomenon* (New York: Viking Adult, 2006).

4. See their 2006 Christmas messages to this network: http://edge
   .org/documents/archive/edge199.html. The contents of all Web
   pages noted in this book have been archived for the purposes of
   verification.

5. Gary Wolf, "The Church of the Non-Believers," *Wired*,
   November 2006: http://www.wired.com/wired/archive/14.11
   /atheism_pr.html. See also Simon Hooper, "The Rise of the
   "New Atheists," *CNN.com*, 9 November 2006: http://edition
   .cnn.com/2006/WORLD/europe/11/08/atheism.feature/index
   .html.

6. Christopher Hitchens, *God Is Not Great: How Religion Poisons
   Everything* (New York: Hachette Book Group, 2007).

7. The phrase *the Four Horsemen* seems first to have been used in
   a discussion between the four writers recorded in 2007. The
   reference is to the biblical image of the Four Horsemen of the
   Apocalypse (Revelation 6:1–8), generally seen as a portent of the
   end times. Other names are often linked with the movement: for
   example, the physicist Victor J. Stenger, who argues that science
   disproves the existence of God (Victor J. Stenger, *God: The Failed
   Hypothesis—How Science Shows That God Does Not Exist* [Amherst,
   NY: Prometheus Books, 2008]). This lumbering book is something of a blunt instrument compared with those by Dawkins or
   Hitchens, even if it echoes at least some of their ideas.

8. Harris, *End of Faith*, 110.

9. Ibid., 109.

10. For the full text of Atran's critique of Harris and others, see
    http://edge.org/discourse/bb.html#atran2.

11. Mark Juergensmeyer, *Terror in the Mind of God: The Global Rise of*

Religious Violence, 3rd ed. (Berkeley, CA: University of California Press, 2003).

12. William T. Cavanaugh, *The Myth of Religious Violence* (Oxford: Oxford University Press, 2009).

13. Ibid., 18–54, 212–20.

14. Ibid., 225.

15. Harris, *End of Faith*, 52–53.

16. See Rudolph J. Rummel, *Lethal Politics: Soviet Genocide and Mass Murder Since 1917* (New Brunswick, NJ: Transaction Publishers, 1990), 109–26.

17. See, for example, R. J. [Richard] Eskow, "Reject Arguments for Intolerance—Even from Atheists," *Huffington Post*, 4 January 2006.

18. Sam Harris, *Letter to a Christian Nation* (New York: Knopf, 2006).

19. Marcia Z. Nelson, "Bestsellers from the Academy," *Publisher's Weekly 253*, no. 46 (November 2006): 20.

20. Sam Harris, *The Moral Landscape: How Science Can Determine Human Values* (New York: Free Press, 2010).

21. Richard Dawkins, *The God Delusion* (London: Bantam, 2006), 5.

22. Ibid.

23. Richard Dawkins, *The Selfish Gene*, 2nd ed. (Oxford: Oxford University Press, 1989), 198.

24. Dawkins, *God Delusion*, 5.

25. Ibid., 308.

26. Michael Shermer, *How We Believe: Science, Skepticism, and the Search for God* (New York: Freeman, 2000), 71.

27. For a very positive assessment of Dawkins's role as a scientific popularizer, see the collection of essays in Alan Grafen

and Mark Ridley, eds., *Richard Dawkins: How a Scientist Changed the Way We Think* (Oxford: Oxford University Press, 2006).

28. I offer an evaluation of Dawkins's views on the relation of science and religion, based on works published up to 2003, in Alister E. McGrath, *Dawkins' God: Genes, Memes, and the Meaning of Life* (Oxford: Blackwell, 2004).

29. Dawkins, *God Delusion*, 188.

30. I discuss this point more fully elsewhere: see Alister E. McGrath, *Darwinism and the Divine: Evolutionary Thought and Natural Theology* (Oxford: Blackwell, 2011), 254–67.

31. See especially Richard Dawkins, *The Blind Watchmaker: Why the Evidence of Evolution Reveals a Universe Without Design* (New York: Norton, 1986).

32. Ibid.

33. Richard Dawkins, "Viruses of the Mind," in *A Devil's Chaplain: Reflections on Hope, Lies, Science and Love* (New York: Mariner Books, 2004), 128–45.

34. Ibid., 144–45.

35. For the origins and early development of this idea, see McGrath, *Dawkins' God*, 119–38.

36. Dawkins, *A Devil's Chaplain*, 145.

37. For an up-to-date account, see McGrath, *Darwinism and the Divine*, 254–62.

38. http://cfpm.org/jom-emit/2005/vol9/edmonds_b.html.

39. Anthony Kenny, *What I Believe* (London: Continuum, 2006), 21.

40. Daniel C. Dennett, *Darwin's Dangerous Idea: Evolution and the Meaning of Life* (New York: Simon & Schuster, 1995).

41. Daniel C. Dennett, *Breaking the Spell: Religion as a Natural Phenomenon* (New York: Viking Penguin, 2006).

42. Ibid., 9.

43. Ibid., 240–46.

44. Ibid., 240.

45. See Keith Ward, *Why There Almost Certainly Is a God: Doubting Dawkins* (Oxford: Lion Hudson, 2008).

46. For some critical reflections see Justin L. Barrett, "Is the Spell Really Broken? Bio-Psychological Explanations of Religion and Theistic Belief," *Theology and Science* 5 (2007), 57–72.

47. Dennett, *Breaking the Spell*, 31–32.

48. Tina Beattie, *The New Atheists: The Twilight of Reason and the War on Religion* (London: Darton, Longman & Todd, 2007), 7–9.

49. Christopher Hitchens, *God Is Not Great: How Religion Poisons Everything* (New York: Twelve, 2007), 13.

50. As cited in Ian Parker's profile of Christopher Hitchens, "He knew he was right," *New Yorker*, 16 October 2006.

51. Hitchens, *God Is Not Great*, 13, 25.

52. For the way in which celebrity can give rise to a certain type of Godlike authority and opinions, see Pete Ward, *Gods Behaving Badly: Media, Religion, and Celebrity Culture* (Waco, TX: Baylor University Press, 2011).

53. George M. Marsden, *A Short Life of Jonathan Edwards* (Grand Rapids, MI: Eerdmans, 2008), 131.

54. Hitchens, *God Is Not Great*, 7.

55. Ibid., 176.

2. What's "New" About the New Atheism?

1. Gary Wolf, "The Church of the Non-Believers," *Wired*, November 2006: http://www.wired.com/wired/archive/14.11 /atheism_pr.html.

2. For recent examples of this diversity, all published after the appearance of the New Atheism, see Steve Antinoff, *Spiritual Atheism* (Berkeley, CA: Counterpoint Press, 2010); André Comte-Sponville, *The Little Book of Atheist Spirituality* (New York: Viking, 2009); J. Angelo Corlett, *The Errors of Atheism* (London: Continuum, 2010).

3. Carlo Maria Martini and Umberto Eco, *Belief or Nonbelief?* (New York: Arcade Publications, 2001).

4. The classic study of this remains E. Digby Baltzell, *The Protestant Establishment: Aristocracy and Caste in America* (New Haven, CT: Yale University Press, 1987). For feminist perspectives on the maleness of leading New Atheists, see Beattie, *The New Atheists*, 126–28. As has often been pointed out, there are surprisingly few African-American atheists.

5. Christopher Hitchens, *Letters to a Young Contrarian* (New York: Basic Books, 2001), 55.

6. Greg M. Epstein, "Less Anti-theism, More Humanism," *Washington Post*, 1 October 2007.

7. Christopher Hitchens in dialogue with Dennis Miller, 30 October 2009. For Hitchens's apology, see http://current.com/shows /upstream/91393992_atheist-christopher-hitchens-apologizes-for -mother-teresa-insult.htm. For his earlier critique, see Christopher Hitchens, *The Missionary Position: Mother Teresa in Theory and Practice* (London: Verso, 1995).

8. From Ian Parker's profile of Christopher Hitchens, "He knew he was right," *New Yorker*, 16 October 2006.

9. Peter L. Berger, *A Far Glory: The Quest for Faith in an Age of Credulity* (New York: Free Press, 1992), 125–26.

10. http://richarddawkins.net/.

11. Figures as of May 2010.

12. This survey was based on 1,648 adults chosen randomly from across the United States, designed by the Baylor Institute for Studies of Religion and conducted by the Gallup organization. For details, see Rodney Stark, *What Americans Really Believe: New Findings from the Baylor Surveys of Religion* (Waco, TX: Baylor University Press, 2008).

13. For example, the majority of Americans who claim to be irreligious pray, with a large minority (32 percent) praying "often."

14. See, for example, Alvin L. Reid, *Radically Unchurched: Who They Are and How to Reach Them* (Grand Rapids, MI: Kregel, 2002); Thom S. Rainer, *The Unchurched Next Door* (Grand Rapids, MI: Zondervan, 2003).

15. http://friendlyatheist.com/2010/02/03/how-many-copies -of-the-god-delusion-have-been-sold/.

16. Bruce DeSilva, "Pundit Christopher Hitchens picks a fight in book, 'God Is Not Great,'" *Rutland Herald* [Vermont], 25 April 2007.

17. Julian Baggini, *A Very Short Introduction to Atheism* (Oxford: Oxford University Press, 2003). This was published before the phenomenon of the New Atheism emerged.

18. Julian Baggini, "Nyateismen virker mot sin hensikt," *Fri Tanke* (March 2009), 42–43.

19. For the English text of this article, see http://www.fritanke.no /ENGLISH/2009/The_new_atheist_movement_is_destructive/.

20. http://julianbaggini.blogspot.com/2009/03/new-atheist -movement-is-destructive.html.

21. Baggini here alludes to the titles of two of the canonical works of the New Atheism, discussed in chapter 1: Richard Dawkins, *The God Delusion* and Daniel Dennett, *Breaking the Spell*.

22. A similar approach is found in Graham R. Oppy, *Arguing About Gods* (Cambridge: Cambridge University Press, 2006). Oppy's point is that while neither atheism nor theism are rationally compelling, they're both nevertheless rational.

23. http://realityismyreligion.wordpress.com/2010/02/23 /locked-entry-will-open-soon/.

24. This posting has since been removed from the Dawkins Web site. It can be accessed, along with other views on this incident, from sites such as http://heathen-hub.com/blog.php?b=254.

25. See, for example, the comments at http://realityismyreligion .wordpress.com/2010/02/23/locked-entry-will-open-soon /#comment-89.

26. Alexander Pope, *Imitations of Horace*, ii.1.

27. For some of the issues relating to anonymity on the Web, see Judith S. Donath, "Identity and Deception in the Virtual Community," in Marc A. Smith and Peter Kollock, eds., *Communities in Cyberspace* (London: Routledge, 1999), 29–59.

28. http://www.courthousenews.com/2010/10/22/31283.htm. For comment, see http://www.independent.co.uk/news/world /americas/an-ungodly-row-at-the-dawkins-foundation-2115632 .html.

29. http://joshtimonen.com/post/1387207318/the-ultimate-betrayal.

30. See Graeme Turner, *Understanding Celebrity* (London: Sage, 2004).

31. Alister McGrath, *The Dawkins Delusion? Atheist Fundamentalism and the Denial of the Divine* (Downers Grove, IL: InterVarsity Press, 2007).

32. http://www.zazzle.co.uk/what_would_dawkins_do _tshirt-235812038105228356. The slogan is a parody of a popular Christian armband reading "WWJD" ("What would Jesus do?").

33. http://smashingtelly.com/2008/06/19/the-four-horsemen -dennett-dawkins-harris-hitchens/.

34. http://news.independentminds.livejournal.com/3760686.html. Viewed and archived 21 June 2010, This page has since been deleted.

35. Daniel C. Dennett, "The Bright Stuff," *New York Times*, 12 July 2003; Richard Dawkins, "The Future Looks Bright," *Guardian*, 21 June 2003.

36. Gary Wolf, "The Church of the Non-Believers," *Wired*, 2006, http://www.wired.com/wired/archive/14.11/atheism_pr.html.

37. http://www.meetup.com/London-Brights/calendar/past_list/.

38. http://www.meetup.com/London-Brights/calendar/4923638/.

39. The London Atheists, who occasionally held joint meetups with the London Brights, continue to function. Their Web site points to ongoing attendance of 12–20 at their recent meetups, somewhat lower than the highs of 2006–7. See http://www .meetup.com/London-Atheists/.

40. Chris Mooney, "Not too 'bright': Richard Dawkins and Daniel Dennett are smart guys, but their campaign to rename religious unbelievers 'Brights' could use some rethinking," *Skeptical Inquirer*, March–April 2004.

41. Christopher Hitchens, *God Is Not Great: How Religion Poisons Everything* (New York: Twelve, 2007), 5.

42. Richard Dawkins, *The God Delusion* (London: Bantam, 2006), 257.

43. Ibid., 259.

3. Violence: When Religion Goes Wrong

1. William Temple, *Nature, Man and God* (London: Macmillan, 1934), 22.

2. For further exploration of this point, see Peter Harrison, *"Religion" and the Religions in the English Enlightenment* (Cambridge: Cambridge University Press, 1990); Daniel L. Pals, *Seven Theories of Religion* (New York: Oxford University Press, 1996); Samuel J. Preus, *Explaining Religion: Criticism and Theory from Bodin to Freud* (New Haven, CT: Yale University Press, 1987).

3. Christopher Hitchens, *Letters to a Young Contrarian* (New York: Basic Books, 2001), 55.

4. Meera Nanda, "Spirited Away," *New Humanist* 121, no. 3, May/June 2006 http://newhumanist.org.uk/973/spirited-away.

5. Ibid.

6. Paul Heelas, Linda Woodhead, Benjamin Seel and Bronislaw Szerszynski, *The Spiritual Revolution: Why Religion Is Giving Way to Spirituality* (Oxford: Blackwell, 2005).

7. Natalya Sadomskaya, "Soviet Anthropology and Contemporary Rituals," *Cahiers du monde russe et soviétique* 31 (1990), 245–53.

8. Martin E. Marty with Jonathan Moore, *Politics, Religion, and the Common Good: Advancing a Distinctly American Conversation About Religion's Role in Our Shared Life* (San Francisco: Jossey-Bass, 2000).

9. Emilio Gentile, *Politics as Religion* (Princeton, NJ: Princeton University Press, 2006), 1–15.

10. Diego Gambetta, ed., *Making Sense of Suicide Missions* (Oxford: Oxford University Press, 2005).

11. Robert A. Pape, *Dying to Win: The Strategic Logic of Suicide Terrorism* (New York: Random House, 2005).

12. Scott Atran, "The Moral Logic and Growth of Suicide Terrorism," *Washington Quarterly* 29:2 (Spring 2006), 127–47.

13. Richard E. Wentz, *Why People Do Bad Things in the Name of Religion* (Macon, GA: Mercer University Press, 1993). See also Sudhir Kakar, *The Colors of Violence: Cultural Identities, Religion, and Conflict* (Chicago: University of Chicago Press, 1996).

14. Alberto Toscano, *Fanaticism: On the Uses of an Idea* (London: Verso, 2010).

15. For exploration of this theme, see Richard A. Burridge, *Imitating Jesus: An Inclusive Approach to New Testament Ethics* (Grand Rapids, MI: Eerdmans, 2007).

16. One of the best recent studies is Walter Wink, *Jesus and Nonviolence: A Third Way* (Minneapolis, MN: Fortress Press, 2003).

17. For an outstanding account of this tragic incident and its implications, see Donald B. Kraybill, Steven M. Nolt, and David Weaver-Zercher, *Amish Grace: How Forgiveness Transcended Tragedy* (San Francisco, CA: Jossey-Bass, 2010). For a more popular account, see Jonas Beiler with Shawn Smucker, *Think No Evil: Inside the Story of the Amish Schoolhouse Shooting—and Beyond* (New York: Howard Books, 2009).

18. The French Revolution went through an atheist phase, but this

did not last long enough to become institutionally embodied in national policy.

19. V. I. Lenin, "Socialism and Religion," in *Collected Works*, 45 vols. (Moscow: Progress Publishers, 1965), 10:83–87.

20. Anna Dickinson, "Quantifying Religious Oppression: Russian Orthodox Church Closures and Repression of Priests 1917–41," *Religion, State and Society* 28 (2000), 327–35. See further Dimitry V. Pospielovsky, *A History of Marxist-Leninist Atheism and Soviet Anti-Religious Policies* (New York: St Martin's Press, 1987); William Husband, "Soviet Atheism and Russian Orthodox Strategies of Resistance, 1917–1932," *Journal of Modern History* 70 (1998), 74–107.

21. Also known as the "League of the Militant Godless." For its history and methods, see Daniel Peris, *Storming the Heavens: The Soviet League of the Militant Godless* (Ithaca, NY: Cornell University Press, 1998). For reflections on the failure of Soviet strategy, see Paul Froese, "Forced Secularization in Soviet Russia: Why an Atheistic Monopoly Failed," *Journal for the Scientific Study of Religion* 43 (2004), 35–50.

22. Christopher Hitchens, *God Is Not Great: How Religion Poisons Everything* (New York: Twelve, 2007), 243–47.

23. Perhaps the most interesting critique of Hitchens's views on the Soviet Union comes from within his own family. Peter Hitchens, brother to Christopher, served for many years as a journalist in the Communist bloc of Eastern Europe. He ended up working in Moscow on the eve of the collapse of the Soviet Union. See Peter Hitchens, *The Rage Against God* (London: Continuum, 2010).

24. Richard Dawkins, *The God Delusion* (London: Bantam, 2006), 273.

25. Ibid., 249.

26. Timothy J. Colton, *Moscow: Governing the Socialist Metropolis* (Cambridge, MA: Harvard University Press, 1995), 228–31.

27. For the story, see Rüdiger Lux and Martin Petzoldt, eds., *Vernichtet, vertrieben—aber nicht ausgelöscht: Gedenken an die Sprengung der Universitätskirche St. Pauli zu Leipzig nach 40 Jahren* (Berlin: Kirchhof & Franke, 2008).

28. Gentile, *Politics as Religion*, 1.

29. François Furet, *The French Revolution, 1770–1814* (Oxford: Blackwell, 1996).

30. "La terreur n'est autre chose que la justice prompte, sévère, inflexible; elle est donc une émanation de la vertu." Maximilien Robespierre, speech entitled "Sur les principes de morale politique qui doivent guider la Convention nationale," delivered 5 February 1794. *Oeuvres de Maximilien Robespierre*, 10 vols. (Enghien les Bains: Editions du Miraval, 2007), 10:357.

31. Terry Eagleton, "Lunging, Flailing, Mispunching," review of *The God Delusion*. *London Review of Books* 28, no. 20 (19 October 2006).

4. Reason: The Rationality of Beliefs

1. John Locke, *Works*, 10 vols. (London: Thomas Tegg, 1823), 8:447.

2. Dante Alighieri, *The Divine Comedy*, "Paradise," 2.56–8.

3. J. J. C. Smart and J. J. Haldane, *Atheism and Theism*, 2nd ed. (Oxford: Blackwell, 2003). At the time of writing, Smart is emeritus professor of philosophy at Monash University, Australia; Haldane is professor of philosophy at St. Andrew's University, Scotland.

4. For a recent study emphasizing the importance of the stability of beliefs in Hume's philosophy see Louis E. Loeb, *Stability and Justification in Hume's Treatise* (Oxford: Oxford University Press, 2002).

5. See, for example, Alvin Plantinga, "Reason and Belief in God" in *Faith and Philosophy: Reason and Belief in God*, ed. Alvin Plantinga and Nicholas Wolterstorff (Notre Dame: University of Notre Dame, 1983), 16–93.

6. Extract from a lecture given by Dawkins at the Edinburgh International Science Festival (1992). The lecture was published under the title "Lions 10, Christians Nil" in an electronic journal entitled "The Nullafidian," http://www.skepticfiles.org/nullif /v01i08.htm.

7. Isaiah Berlin, *Concepts and Categories: Philosophical Essays* (New York: Viking Press, 1979), 2–5, 161–62.

8. Ibid., 114–15.

9. Terry Eagleton, "Lunging, Flailing, Mispunching," review of *The God Delusion, London Review of Books* 28, no. 20 (19 October 2006).

10. Alvin Plantinga, *God and Other Minds: A Study of the Rational Justification of Belief in God* (Ithaca, NY: Cornell University Press, 1990).

11. James H. Olthuis, "On Worldviews" in *Stained Glass: Worldviews and Social Science*, ed. Paul A. Marshall (Lanham, MD: University Press of America, 1989), 26–32.

12. Christopher Hitchens, *God Is Not Great: How Religion Poisons Everything* (New York: Twelve, 2007), 5.

13. See M. Neil Browne and Stuart M. Keeley, *Asking the Right*

Questions: A Guide to Critical Thinking, 8th ed. (Upper Saddle River, NJ: Pearson Prentice Hall, 2007), 196.

14. See especially Robert J. Louden, *The World We Want: How and Why the Ideals of the Enlightenment Still Elude Us* (Oxford: Oxford University Press, 2007).

15. Richard Dawkins, *The God Delusion* (London: Bantam, 2006), 31.

16. This point was made by Xenophon in the classical period. The modern origins of this approach lie in Ludwig Feuerbach: see Van A. Harvey, *Feuerbach and the Interpretation of Religion* (Cambridge: Cambridge University Press, 1995).

17. See Heinz Fastenrath, *Ein Abriss atheistischer Grundpositionen: Feuerbach, Marx, Nietzsche, Sartre* (Stuttgart: Klett, 1993). For the background to these developments, see Winfried Schröder, *Ursprünge des Atheismus: Untersuchungen zur Metaphysik- und Religionskritik des 17. und 18. Jahrhunderts* (Stuttgart-Bad Cannstatt: Frommann-Holzboog, 1998).

18. Hitchens, *God Is Not Great*, 8.

19. Ibid., 10.

20. Alexander Pope, *Essay on Man*, 1.

21. Hitchens, *God Is Not Great*, 102.

22. Iris Murdoch, "The Sovereignty of Good over Other Concepts" in *Existentialists and Mystics*, ed. Peter Conradi (London: Chatto, 1998), 363–85.

23. Iris Murdoch, *Henry and Cato* (London: Triad, 1977), 135.

24. See, for example, Alister E. McGrath, "Atheism and the Enlightenment: Reflections on the Intellectual Roots of the New Atheism" in *The Passionate Intellect: Christian Faith and the Discipleship of the Mind* (Downers Grove, IL: InterVarsityPress, 2010), 169–85.

25. For excellent studies, see Jeffrey Stout, *The Flight from Authority: Religion, Morality and the Quest for Autonomy* (Notre Dame: University of Notre Dame Press, 1981); Maiken Umbach, *Federalism and Enlightenment in Germany, 1740–1806* (London: Hambledon Press, 2000); Gertrude Himmelfarb, *The Roads to Modernity: The British, French and American Enlightenments* (New York: Knopf, 2005); Jonathan I. Israel, *Enlightenment Contested: Philosophy, Modernity, and the Emancipation of Man, 1670–1752* (Oxford: Oxford University Press, 2008).

26. Rebecca Goldstein, *The Proof and Paradox of Kurt Gödel* (New York: Norton, 1995), 204.

27. See, for example, Alasdair MacIntyre, *Whose Justice? Which Rationality?* (London: Duckworth, 1988); Stephen Toulmin, *Cosmopolis: The Hidden Agenda of Modernity* (New York: Free Press, 1990); John Gray, *Enlightenment's Wake: Politics and Culture at the Close of the Modern Age* (London: Routledge, 1995).

28. William James, "The Sentiment of Rationality" in *The Will to Believe and Other Essays in Popular Philosophy* (New York: Longmans, Green and Co., 1897), 63–110.

29. The classic study remains Bernhard Kopp, "Die marxistische Theorie von Überbau und Unterbau und ihre nicht-marxistischen Abwandlungen," *Zeitschrift für philosophische Forschung* 22 (1968), 575–97.

30. I have in mind here Johann Georg Hamann's late eighteenth-century critique of Kant, which involves the recognition that "knowers" are shaped by their cultural context: see Oswald Bayer, *Vernunft ist Sprache: Hamanns Metakritik Kants* (Stuttgart: Frommann-Holzboog, 2002).

31. Daniel C. Dennett, *Darwin's Dangerous Idea: Evolution and the Meaning of Life* (New York: Simon & Schuster, 1995), 63.

32. Stephen P. Stich, *The Fragmentation of Reason: Preface to a Pragmatic Theory of Cognitive Evaluation* (Cambridge, MA: MIT Press, 1990), 62.

33. Hitchens, *God Is Not Great*, 283.

34. It is not my intention to explore the Christian view of this matter, but informed readers will immediately realize that both the New Testament and the Christian tradition recognize and engage precisely this point. We do not see and think clearly; we need illumination and grace. For the classic discussion of this idea in Augustine of Hippo, see Robert J. Hardy, *Actualité de la révélation divine* (Paris: Éditions Beauchesne, 1974), 60–68.

35. See Jeremy Gray, *Ideas of Space: Euclidean, Non-Euclidean, and Relativistic*, 2nd ed. (Oxford: Clarendon Press, 1989).

36. A point emphasized in MacIntyre, *Whose Justice? Which Rationality?*

5. Science: A Question of Proof

1. Thomas H. Huxley, *Darwiniana* (London: Macmillan, 1893), 252.

2. Hugh G. Gauch, *Scientific Method in Practice* (New York: Cambridge University Press, 2003), 1–110.

3. The best study is Peter Lipton, *Inference to the Best Explanation*, 2nd ed. (London: Routledge, 2004).

4. Mary B. Hesse, *Forces and Fields: The Concept of Action at a Distance in the History of Physics* (London: Nelson, 2005).

5. See the points made in James T. Cushing, *Quantum Mechanics:*

Historical Contingency and the Copenhagen Hegemony (Chicago: University of Chicago Press, 1994).

6. For the debate and the issues, see the collection of essays in Bernard Carr, ed., *Universe or Multiverse?* (Cambridge: Cambridge University Press, 2007).

7. Helge S. Kragh, *Conceptions of Cosmos: From Myths to the Accelerating Universe: A History of Cosmology* (Oxford: Oxford University Press, 2006).

8. Richard Dawkins, "Darwin Triumphant," in *A Devil's Chaplain: Reflections on Hope, Lies, Science, and Love* (New York: Mariner Books, 2004), 78–90.

9. Thomas S. Kuhn, *The Structure of Scientific Revolutions* (Chicago: University of Chicago Press, 1962), 10.

10. Richard Dawkins, *The Selfish Gene*, 2nd ed. (Oxford: Oxford University Press, 1989), 330.

11. For a collection of essays from leading thinkers exploring the options, see Carr, ed., *Universe or Multiverse?*

12. See, for example, the important discussion of the relation between *evidence* and *warrant* in Susan Haack, *Evidence and Inquiry* (Oxford: Blackwell, 1993).

13. James Robert Brown, *Philosophy of Mathematics: An Introduction to the World of Proofs and Pictures* (London: Routledge, 1999), 71–78; George Boolos, "Gödel's Second Incompleteness Theorem Explained in Words of One Syllable," *Mind* 103 (1994), 1–3.

14. For a highly influential discussion, see John Lucas, "Minds, Machines and Gödel," *Philosophy* 36 (1961), 112–27.

15. See his famous comments on F. W. Hutton's concerns about his

theory: *The Life and Letters of Charles Darwin*, ed. F. Darwin, 3 vols. (London: John Murray, 1887), 2:155.

16. Pietro Corsi, "Before Darwin: Transformist Concepts in European Natural History," *Journal of the History of Biology* 38 (2005), 67–83.

17. For a discussion of these difficulties, see Abigail J. Lustig, "Darwin's Difficulties." In the *Cambridge Companion to the "Origin of Species*," eds. Michael Ruse and Robert J. Richards (Cambridge: Cambridge University Press, 2009), 109–28.

18. See Michael Bulmer, "Did Jenkins's Swamping Argument Invalidate Darwin's Theory of Natural Selection?" *British Journal for the History of Science* 37 (2004), 281–97.

19. Charles Darwin, *Origin of Species* (London: John Murray, 1859), 171.

20. Gauch, *Scientific Method in Practice*, 152.

21. Julia Kristeva, *The Incredible Need to Believe* (New York: Columbia University Press, 2009), 3. Her general point is widely accepted within contemporary philosophy: see for example, Slavoj Žižek, *How to Read Lacan* (London: Granta, 2007), 93–94; John Cottingham, *Why Believe?* (London: Continuum, 2009).

22. Bas C. van Fraassen, *The Scientific Image* (Oxford: Oxford University Press, 1980), 202–3.

23. Dawkins, "Science, Genetics and Ethics" in *A Devil's Chaplain*, 27–37.

24. John Dupré, "Against Scientific Imperialism," *PSA: Proceedings of the Biennial Meeting of the Philosophy of Science Association* 2 (1994), 374–81.

25. For critiques see Frederick A. Olafson, *Naturalism and the Human Condition: Against Scientism* (London: Routledge, 2001); Mikael Stenmark, *Scientism: Science, Ethics and Religion* (Aldershot: Ashgate,

2001). For helpful nuancing of the issues, see Susan Haack, *Defending Science—Within Reason: Between Scientism and Cynicism* (Amherst, NY: Prometheus Books, 2003).

26. Hilary Putnam, "Was Wittgenstein Really an Anti-Realist about Mathematics?" in *Wittgenstein in America*, ed. Timothy C. McCarthy and Sean C. Stidd (Oxford: Oxford University Press, 2001), 140–94; quote at 185–86.

27. Sam Harris, *The Moral Landscape: How Science Can Determine Human Values* (New York: Free Press, 2010).

28. See especially the analysis in Ruth Anna Putnam, "Perceiving Facts and Values," *Philosophy* 73, no. 283 (1998), 5–19. Putnam here points out the implicit subjectivism intrinsic to any "scientific" attempt to achieve ethical objectivity.

29. See, for example, the insightful *New York Times* review of the work: Kwame Anthony Appiah, "Science knows best," *New York Times*, 1 October 2010.

30. Peter B. Medawar, *The Limits of Science* (Oxford: Oxford University Press, 1985), 66.

31. Stephen Jay Gould, "Impeaching a Self-Appointed Judge," *Scientific American* 267, no. 1 (1992), 118–21.

32. Thomas Dixon, "Scientific Atheism as a Faith Tradition," *Studies in History and Philosophy of Science C* 33 (2002), 337–59.

33. Jeffrey Burton Russell, *Inventing the Flat Earth: Columbus and Modern Historians* (New York: Praeger, 1991).

34. The best study is John Hedley Brooke, *Science and Religion: Some Historical Perspectives* (Cambridge: Cambridge University Press, 1991).

35. For the role of this Institute in developing Soviet genetics, see A. E. Gaissinovitch, "The Origins of Soviet Genetics and the

Struggle with Lamarckism, 1922–1929," *Journal for the History of Biology* 13 (1980), 1–51.

36. Dimitry V. Pospielovsky, *A History of Marxist–Leninist Atheism and Soviet Anti-Religious Policies*, 2 vols. (New York: St Martin's Press, 1987).

37. See, for example, the recent studies of David B. Wilson, "The Historiography of Science and Religion" in Gary B. Ferngren, ed., *Science and Religion: A Historical Introduction* (Baltimore: Johns Hopkins University Press, 2002), 13–39; Thomas Dixon, G. N. Cantor, and Stephen Pumfrey, eds., *Science and Religion: New Historical Perspectives* (Cambridge: Cambridge University Press, 2010).

38. See Ronald L. Numbers, ed., *Galileo Goes to Jail and Other Myths About Science and Religion* (Cambridge, MA: Harvard University Press, 2009).

39. Dawkins, *The God Delusion*, 66–69.

40. Paul Parson, "How to Sell Science to the Big Brother Generation," *New Scientist*, 3 December 2008.

41. http://richarddawkins.net/articles/3382.

42. The debate was transmitted by the BBC on its then Third Programme, a channel dedicated to serious cultural issues. It remains a landmark in contemporary discussion. For the text of the debate, see Al Seckel, *Bertrand Russell on God and Religion* (Buffalo, NY: Prometheus Books, 1986), 123–46.

43. For a good popular account, see Simon Singh, *Big Bang: The Origin of the Universe* (New York: Fourth Estate, 2004).

44. See Stan Wallace, ed., *Does God Exist? The Craig–Flew Debate* (Aldershot: Ashgate, 2003).

45. For his own account of his turnaround on this issue, see Antony Flew, *There Is a God* (New York: HarperOne, 2007). Dawkins is singularly ungracious about this development, dismissing it as an "over-publicized tergiversation" on the part of a minor senile philosopher: Dawkins, *The God Delusion*, 92.

46. For a detailed account and interpretation of these phenomena, see Alister E. McGrath, *A Fine-Tuned Universe: The Quest for God in Science and Theology* (Louisville, KY: Westminster John Knox Press, 2009).

47. Fred Hoyle, "The Universe: Past and Present Reflections," *Annual Review of Astronomy and Astrophysics* 20 (1982), 1–35.

48. For a discussion of this point, see Alister E. McGrath, *Surprised by Meaning: Science, Faith, and How We Make Sense of Things* (Louisville, KY: Westminster John Knox Press, 2011).

49. Isaiah Berlin, *The Crooked Timber of Humanity: Chapters in the History of Ideas* (London: Pimlico, 2003), 208–13. The curious title of this important collection of essays reflects a famous dictum of Immanuel Kant: "Nothing straight was ever made out of the crooked timber of humanity."

50. The importance of this point is noted by John Pennington, "The 'Childish Imagination' of John Ruskin and George Macdonald: Introductory Speculations," *North Wind* 16 (1997), 55–65.

51. For a recording of the debate, see http://fixed-point.org /index.phpvideo/35-full-length/164-the-dawkins-lennox -debate.

52. http://richarddawkins.net/audio/1707-debate-between-richard -dawkins-and-john-lennox.

6. Where Is the New Atheism Now?

1. *Oxford Student*, 19 May 2010. "Prominent writer and commentator Christopher Hitchens described the Archbishop of Canterbury as a 'sheep-faced loon' at a debate on secularism in Oxford on 12 May."

2. For example, in his interview with Simon Mayo on BBC Radio Five, broadcast on 18 June 2007. This comment, which shocked Mayo, generated delight for many New Atheist bloggers. Others were alarmed at the obvious damage such comments caused to the public image of the New Atheism. See http://richarddawkins.net/audio/1304-interview-with-richard-dawkins.

3. Charles A. Shriner, *Wit, Wisdom and Foibles of the Great* (New York: Funk & Wagnalls, 1918), 567.

4. "Richard Dawkins calls for arrest of Pope Benedict XVI." *Sunday Times* (London), April 11, 2010.

5. Richard Dawkins, "Ratzinger Is the Perfect Pope," *Washington Post*, March 28, 2010.

6. *Independent*, 21 September 2010. See also the same newspaper's leading article "Benedict spoke to Britain," 20 September 2010.

7. Barbara Bradley Hagarty, "A Bitter Rift Divides Atheists," *National Public Radio*, 19 October 2009. Text at http://www.npr.org/templates/story/story.php?storyId=113889251.

8. See Paul Kurtz, *What is Secular Humanism?* (Amherst, NY: Prometheus Books, 2006).

9. For the text, see http://www.americanhumanist.org/Who_We_Are/About_Humanism/Humanist_Manifesto_II.

10. http://community.beliefnet.com/go/thread/view/43861

/18728697/Ron_Lindsay_Steals_Center_for_Inquiry_from
_Paul_Kurtz.

11. Mark Oppenheimer, "Closer Look at Rift Between Humanists Reveals Deeper Divisions," *New York Times*, 1 October 2010.

12. Paul Kurtz, "The 'True Unbeliever,'" *Free Inquiry* 30/1 (December 2009/January 2010), http://www.secularhumanism .org/index.php?section=library&page=kurtz_fi_30_1 (the italics are Kurtz's).

13. Ibid.

7. God Won't Go Away: Beyond the New Atheism

1. Christopher Hitchens, *The Missionary Position: Mother Teresa in Theory and Practice* (London: Verso, 1995).

2. Christopher Hitchens, *God Is Not Great: How Religion Poisons Everything* (New York: Twelve, 2007), 12.

3. William S. Bainbridge and Rodney Stark, *The Future of Religion: Secularization, Revival, and Cult Formation* (Berkeley, CA: University of California Press, 1985), 1.

4. For an excellent study of these trends, see Luke Bretherton, *Christianity and Contemporary Politics: The Conditions and Possibilities of Faithful Witness* (Oxford: Wiley-Blackwell, 2010).

5. Much of Hitchens's argument here is anticipated in John Trenchard's *Natural History of Superstition* (1709).

6. For a survey of recent discussions of this point see Tom Sjöblom, "Spandrels, Gazelles and Flying Buttresses: Religion as Adaptation or as a By-Product," *Journal of Cognition and Culture* 7 (2007), 293–312; McGrath, *Darwinism and the Divine*, 254–67.

7. See Tom Wright, *Simply Christian: Why Christianity Makes Sense* (San Francisco: HarperOne, 2006); Timothy J. Keller, *The Reason for God: Belief in an Age of Skepticism* (New York: Dutton, 2008); Alister E. McGrath, *Surprised by Meaning: Science, Faith, and How We Make Sense of Things* (Louisville, KY: Westminster John Knox Press, 2011).

8. John Haldane, "Philosophy, the Restless Heart, and the Meaning of Theism," *Ratio* 19 (2006), 421–40.

9. Charles Taylor, *A Secular Age* (Cambridge, MA: Harvard University Press, 2007), 530.

10. Bart van Leeuwen and Francisco Lombo de Léon, "Charles Taylor on Secularization," *Ethical Perspectives* 10 (2003), 80–88.

INDEX

arrogance of, 42, 46, 57, 97
attitudes toward, xiii, 35–36, 141
beliefs of, 91
celebrity culture, 51
challenge to core ideas of, 130
characteristics of leading
   representatives of, 35
criticism of, 8, 37, 43, 92, 95,
   136
dogmatism of, 31, 34, 37, 43, 46,
   106, 141
elimination of religion as goal,
   47–48
as embarrassment to atheists, 34
emergence of, xi–xii, 3–4, 146
fanaticism of, 39
internal conflict within, 124
leading representatives of, xiii–
   xiv, 3–33, 36, 57
long-term significance of, 42
movement known as, 153n1
philosophical foundation of,
   25–26
physical meetings and
   communities, 39, 55
questions raised by, xii–xiii
rage against religion by, 119
science and atheism, 120
size of atheist community,
   40–45
skepticism about, 136
viciousness of, 140–142

virtual community of (*see* Web
   sites and blogs)
writings about, sales of, 42
Newton, Isaac, 109
9/11 attacks. *See* September 11, 2001
   attacks
Nonviolence, 69–71

Obama, Barack, 137
Online communities. *See* Web sites
   and blogs
Origin of Species (Darwin), 113
Other minds, 87
Out-groups, 57–58

Pape, Robert, 67–68
Pasteur, Louis, 30
Paulos, John Allen, 57
Peirce, Charles S., 113
Personality cults, 51
Plantinga, Alvin, 84, 87
Pluralism, 64
Polanyi, Michael, 110
Politics
   faith and, 137
   political fanaticism, 67, 69
   as religion, 69
   suicide bombings and, 68
   violence and political
      extremism, 71
Postmodernism, 98
Prayer, 159n13

About the Author

A lister E. McGrath holds the chair of theology, ministry, and education at King's College London, having previously held the chair of historical theology at Oxford University. A former atheist, he has a special interest in dialoguing with and critiquing the New Atheism, and he has publicly debated Richard Dawkins, Daniel Dennett, and Christopher Hitchens. He has written many books, including the international best seller *The Dawkins Delusion?*. He lectures regularly in the United States.